AS IF IT FELL

FROM THE SUN

ISBN: 978-1-4675-1461-3

Cover illustration, Linda Norton, "Answer," 2010, from the series "American Song
    Book (Passerines)"
Cover, interior design, and typesetting by HR Hegnauer

EtherDome Press and its authors extend their thanks and appreciation to the literary
periodicals and presses who have previously published some of the poems in this
anthology. These include but are not limited to the following: Apogee Press, Ahsahta
Press, Litmus Press, *Big Ugly Review, elimae, Lone Mountain Anthology, Ploughshares,
Pool, Turnrow, With+Stand*

EtherDome Chapbooks
(Instance)
San Francisco and Boulder

AS IF IT FELL
FROM THE SUN

An EtherDome Anthology: Ten Years of Women's Writing

Edited by

COLLEEN LOOKINGBILL &

ELIZABETH ROBINSON

INTRODUCTION

We published our first two chapbooks in the year 2000—by most time standards, not so very long ago. Hard to believe all that has happened in this last decade plus, both to our world at large and to our individual lives. It all started innocently enough—a casual conversation with Elizabeth on the telephone. She mentioned that she wanted to do a project with a prescient notion of somehow extending the limits of our known publishing world to others, specifically by doing a series of chapbooks focusing on unpublished writers. I recall the conversation vividly, because it was as though another person was saying the words that were in my own mind. Those words were something like "The problem is, fewer women get published, because women in general are less likely to promote their writing. Less likely to send it out their writing and less likely to even think it is worth sending out!" So it was done—we agreed—we would have a press devoted to chapbooks, limited to women authors who had not yet published a book or chapbook. And we characteristically jumped in with both feet, fueled by good intentions, but not much experience, charmed by the chapbook format, and with a sound enthusiasm for our newfound mission—working with women writers whom we admired and whose work we wanted to share.

Both Colleen and I emerged, albeit in different ways, from generous and vital traditions of experimental writing and small press publishing (in fact, we met in San Francisco in a workshop taught by Dodie Bellamy). How to participate in the ongoing life of that tradition? How to stretch its boundaries? Our growing recognition that there were plenty of fantastic women writers out there who were going mysteriously unpublished catalyzed our project. Living in Bay Area—where such important projects as Kelsey St. Press and *How(ever)* brought significant writing by women into print, meant that we had very helpful exemplars. Rather than a press that published full-length books or a regular periodical, though, we decided to make chapbooks. This seemed like a feasible approach for two people who didn't exactly know what they were doing. In addition, we were paying out of pocket for the project, so it needed to be financially modest enough that we could sustain the costs year after year. Even more than economy, the chapbook betokens a sense of intimacy. It fits nicely in the hand; it offers a smaller, but still representative, selection of the author's work. We determined that we'd each pick one poet to work with each year, making our selections more or less independently of each other, and then launch the work out into the world. And what to call our press? It seemed to me that we needed to pick a name that gestured in gratitude toward women writers whom we admired and whose legacies we feel heir to. I remember I wanted to call the press "Nightwood Chapbooks" after Djuna Barnes, but another press, Nightwood Editions, had beat us to the punch. "EtherDome," then, comes from a poem by Emily Dickinson. I like the way it conjures an open and inclusive space, a site, in this case, for poetry. Poetry by women.

Why, at this juncture, in a community full of accomplished and engaged women writers, would we feel the need to continue the project of running a press that publishes work exclusively by women? I think both Colleen and I know and respect the arguments against essentialism and understand that representation is a slippery, difficult matter. Most of our EtherDome authors are, after all, white (almost universally middle class, most often heterosexual) women. We have tried to push a bit against a tendency we perceive to publish young writers, mixing up generations amongst our authors. This is to confess right off the bat that our claims are modest. We still perceive a need for a particular space in which women can enter the conversation and present their work. E. Tracy Grinnell's comments in an issue of *Aufgabe* speak to some of the same perplexities and dilemmas that Colleen and I have considered:

> Yes, we do numbers with *Aufgabe* because it is impossible not
> to register the lower number of submissions received from

female poets and because it is impossible to separate one's own convictions, aesthetics, and poetic interests from issues of race, class, gender, orientation, and politics in general. We do numbers, however roughly, because each act of editing is an assertion of these positions in some form. The results are mostly imperfect but these things must line up: one cannot claim a progressive and inclusive—and feminist, if truly progressive and inclusive— politics and then proceed to publish serial volumes that fail to represent artists working from a range of circumstances, orientations, or positions. Our politics are essential and we reveal them in every editorial act.

Reading through this anthology, I don't think that we expect you to encounter and thereby define a supremely female poetry. Our very editorial process works against this: each year, Colleen and I have each simply chosen a sample of work that engaged us individually. We didn't even always agree on each other's choices, and that, to me, is part of the hardiness and beauty of our endeavor. The voices of the writers here vary. Their formal decisions, their preoccupations, and their range of curiosity come together within this anthology with a lively, if occasionally dissonant, clatter. Perhaps what we are trying to shape, then, is not an essential women's poetry, but a response to our own sense that a space should be made a bit broader so that women can enter, experiment, find out for themselves what they want their art to do and to be. Chapbooks are terse, tightly framed containers of work. As such, they permit poets to make forays into the provisional, the pleasurable: the *process* that is making art. For me, then, EtherDome is a process that has enhanced my sense of community. Working with Colleen has been a durably meaningful, evolving work of friendship and writing. Similarly, the joys (and occasional exasperations) of working with these writers has continued to mold my participation in a writing community and in discrete works of poetry. I could not ask for better.

Before starting this publishing adventure, I spent a number of years immersing myself in women's writing. In actual fact, I literally did not read any poetry or for that matter, any kind of writing at all, unless it was written by a woman. It was clearly evident for me that my own feminine nature craved and even required women's words - nothing else was possible. In the midst of such definitive self-exploration, to have up close and personal interaction with twenty-one women poets through the design and completion of the chapbook series; each book and each woman unique, original, and talented, was an experience of a lifetime. And partnering with Elizabeth over the extended time of this endeavor was a remarkable collaboration. Publishing, editing and meeting deadlines turned out to be just the right path for us to deepen our connection. You will soon discover for yourself, through this remarkable anthology, representing every writer we published in the last decade, fierce and amazingly evocative poetry that honors the innovative and small press publishing ethos that Elizabeth and I explore in our own writing. Is women's poetry unique in a particular way? This topic has been explored since at least the early seventies, by writers and anthologists with far more knowledge and expertise than me. Whatever your own conclusion, as you read this anthology, we think you will be intrigued and enchanted by writing that weaves an inviting spell of both our material world and the internal world of woman with grace and wit and diverse creativeness. Step into this collection with us as we share with you the expansive fruits of our little publishing project, celebrating ten years of EtherDome chapbooks and the women who made it all possible.

Colleen Lookingbill, Elizabeth Robinson
Editors

WOMEN'S PICTURES

Merle Bachman

                      —the way things fold-up inside her.
a velvet pocket, a locket, a poodle skirt, a flirt

the quality of April light,
a delicate abatement of worries.

the figure of a woman rises, her skin-so-soft, her
hair-so-fresh

light trapped in the slats.
a well-scrubbed infant, a pot boiling, a plain apron, a cigarette
burning out.

inside the woman's body, furrows, pockets, a new idea sprouting
  buds of arms and legs—

chaotic mouth interrupting rain

A mountain waits at the top of the pass for slow-motion dissolve

while the couple in grey and   grosgrain
bury themselves in lavender

a darkening thorax surrounds them. His hands recast her figure in
sugar   for the thousandth time   "magnificent obsession"
    the *mise en scene* of love.   birds trill:

the smell of passion enchants the nearby villagers, out
for an evening stroll on uneven decks
carved of elephant ivory and caramel.

Now, voyager

if you find yourself aboard a cruise ship, then:

    cocktails - butterfly-gowns - gallants

offering to light your cigarette
(as waves all the while bear you to a tropic coast, at night
the engines churning)

how grand to suffer wearing perfect makeup, avec
glycerine eyes
      your feet suddenly fitting

tiny shoes.   big shoulders, limp
hand waving protest
                    ——This exists in the dark. as it should

(while the ship all the while splits the channel

the deepest Atlantic rift no match for what happens :

Under the hovering pearl
of a lens
outsized features of a female face become classical

What is required? that the woman die
or suffer in a transcendent way befitting smoldering
light, sequins beaded in her dress, opalescent issue of
proffered cigarettes?

A gown burns

it must, her flesh
incandescent
on a darkened deck

imagine   a body designed
for love,   the smoke   of it

a sacrifice to keep us   content

adieu

All night thinking when I should have been just dreaming or even
sleeping in my pocket of warmth in a cold house, about her; her soft
mutable face on which the play of expression registers through light. I
suppose only a man could have lit her this way; chosen her for the
shape and paleness of her face, registering as a blank heart amid
opposing banks of colors. The woman must suffer and deny herself, must
enclose herself in a wreath of stiff denials; must wear fitted tweeds
or *crepe de chine* and lady's gloves (and lady's slippers). And flowers
must pour into the car in which she rides, blind over the mountain
passes, heading into the lights of an old town under the wide-eyed moon.

WHAT COMES AFTER

1.

Invoking an old order of things, I sit as the rain

and of course if I were someone a more solid vessel write

in terms of lipstick on burned-down cigarettes or cat hair flecking black

but feeling badly leads to a sense of dismissal, and so viewing all the books

unfolding in soprano, a piece called "sorrowful song of all sorrowful
     song of——"

——tatting or increments of lace, a pungent color, only rain and a milk sky
     surprisingly illuminated

2.

He held me, and this helped to shape the borders of my world.
No guards were posted there, no enemy in sight.
Arms like marble carvings, the most beautiful part
apart from eyes, lips, long jesus-feet.
What is the temper of this time, that he is missing in such
large measure?
The only adequate terms for love rhyme
with sex: fellatio, its creamy sound; cunningulus, a word evoking
language itself,
or
cunning.

3.

The smell of you, the cones of you, the saucers, pipes,
  doors revolving and doors stuck fast

  but especially your density, the vibration in your arms, your hands,

its piercing, the hum inside your thighs, the knee-knobs, ankles

  the smell of you but just the way you
take shape

fill space:

4.

DECEMBER OF BODIES

anthems of marvel
littoral gutteral
glitteral -- *speak to me, musics*
the name inside a dream, utter it
lucidly

all the planets have eyes, wide open

matter not *matter* spill *matter* craft *matter* sprout

a timepiece between   breast and mouth   the gleaming bones are
buried, after all, arrayed around
            our hearts:

sequence: [this matter
of trust]

1

bodily you are a gateway
so am I   sonorous it heaves through us in fountain pink
trembling   contained potential spatter   because dusk must mate
before we do   lingering along tongues entirely its own language
to dart inside each other's gates, a privilege
like the Cochin children of Katamon Tet   their fragrant skins
tea-dark & happy   (I remember)

2

a tingle undergirds the moment   backward bends me over his mat
telephone inside your ear-globe
effervesce me, a postulate of clouds   that early order

centuries inside pulled notes
krishna floats along the milky tide & I'd fain pull
a milk from you   wrapped eagerly alongside each other on thin mattress
13th floor of the 13th apartment on 13th street near avenue D
mystic city

3

an unexpected paleness in   ten o'clock sky   forms photo-negative
amid black branches of molecular tree
braided circumstance in which   we open mouths   scatter a few
        sparks
purring occurs in syncopated
  wandering   (his hands along her
velvet cords)   that hovercraft of glitter!   *play it again, K*
backwards in a warehouse in Lexington   or circular flat where
we sharply   move together--

4

what is   intimacy? the way a mind channels its
   ghost   upstream in word-canoes across
time   into her fever   —but yesterday's warmth converts to particles
ice in the Ohio. withdrawn into our separate nights, everything's a dream
        especially the curvature of   a man's lower lip At the floodwall
down by Story Ave a memory of water lifts
a swollen stream of rotten leaves Dixie cups condoms
a body shifting faintly in sleep   whose arms have yet to hold
whose hands
   to touch

5

a light snow commences
                              wordless oratory
                                              in exchange with
cold sun
                    in bed all day, a possibility   fretting a steel
guitar
                          curtain rises in   the bathtub   she hums a soliloquy
            he sets a scale   on fire   season of scant light   snow suspended
sealing every inch
                        new copper on the roof, a plastic crèche
glows ominous
                    walking alone, the rapid dark

thinking   New York a piñata   far off braceleting a

harbor
                snow accumulation   a raised arm   its pale   fragrance

may i taste you?   a possibility   in exchange with

   a lamb in   the estuary

  season of   gamelan, its icicle wind
                        walking alone

through each other's   bodies

FORFEIT

Faith Barrett

The clock face had been painted to resemble nothing so much as a clock

and she agreed to pretend all the facades were thriving cities,

one hand raised grandly as if to authenticate, seizing days of rain.

Obviously, our raincoats should not have been relied on,

an obdurate "we" which persists, months later,

which resembles nothing so much as impermeable solitude,

one hand raised and seizing grandly, as if to say,

nothing fails like endeavor. Any excuse for a little mirthlessness

where even a flower stand at twilight thrives on gaudy principles.

His mind had relied on itself until late in the day

when the builders came. Miraculous flowers authenticate winter hedges.

What a pity. All the new colors resembled a display.

What's recollected persists and thrives grandly on principle:

Miss Winter Fledgling, Miss Petty Rage.

There were large cars and dark umbrellas, seizing any excuse for solitude, his impermeable mercies and his mother in a gaudy raincoat.

Technically, the rain exaggerates the weather system

as our faces approximate nothing so much as feeling.

What a pity. Any excuse to display our persistent hopes.

Audrey's hand was raised up, to seize him back miraculously,

as if it were too late, a row of empty houses lit up in the rain

where two gaudy beagles pursued their evening purposes

where the persistent flower stand thrived on its display.

No surprise, no surprises. Nothing fails like persistence.

On the telephone, he used a voice he had once reserved for solitude.

One obdurate body riddled with starts and longings relies grandly on itself

until its gaudy gestures begin to resemble a display.

It's too late. So the way he slept did make her angry, did persist,

relying on the clock of solitude, seizing on "we" with exaggerated feeling,

having had our miraculous season of plenty.

Someone came over, but couldn't stay long.

The impermeable billboard grandly declared them "alive with pleasure," in a city which thrived on nothing so much as their resemblance,

their petty authenticities. Someone's boyfriend became miraculously obligated,

so they had to kiss, technically,

the thwarting of the bottle-neck with two gaudy heads.

When his mother pretended to inquire, had he had any breakfast,

women seemed to thrive on being solicitous, to seize on understanding.

Nothing fails like any excuse for success.

One magnetic blunder led to another, on principle.

He put his hand first in one gaudy box, then grandly in the other. Too late.

What a pity. One moment she had disappeared through the door of the jetway,

and the next she was on the freeway, trying to recollect the obvious music,

which resembled nothing so much as turning a blind corner in the brain.

The thrill of exaggerating every failure, Audrey's name overturning the day.

It's the consent of the weary to the seizing of an impermeable wilderness

under winter's excuse for the ruined field. Little did we know.

So irritation persists and with it the authentic tendency to stroke her hair,

seizing on any feeling which pursues itself, which resists.

"WHOSE BIRTHDAY?"

In her bold hand on the jewel case
In permanent ink
What was it she had
In her stylish hand
To get at the permanence of five years
What was it she had said

Whose birthday? was not
In the form of a gift
On the jewel case
She had burned a disk of music
He turned towards her
With a stylish confidence

To get at permanence, to get five years
You may speak for as long as you like
From a red paper box
The stylish chocolates
Wrapped in foil
Were knocked off course

A grandfather clock she left behind
What is it that makes or doesn't
Make things dear
You may stay for as long as you like
Knocks us off our course
In a red paper box whose birthday

What was it she said
A sketch in ink of the telephone niche
The curve of it always empty
As if she might lean
Lean into this longing, with confidence
This I am not permitted

What was it
Made them dear, made them lean in
Arrive at a stylish permanence
In her bold hand
I wish you had more confidence
Wrapped in foil, a red paper box now empty

The permanent shell of an argument
The turtle might go forward or back
Must never catch up
I must not touch it
You may speak if you like
Must not touch its delicate face

Just as the salmon hurl their weight
What might I retain, what can I take
Up through the water, up the falls
From your persistent retreat
Trying so doggedly to press upstream
The delicate niche of its permanence

Maybe autumn is the season
How could I have mistaken
Thrashing upstream

His carapace of solitude
Must not settle in
To the lush weight of her confidence

For mine. This is their history.
The tangle of his hands
But I'm right up close whose birthday
I am not permitted
A niche of arrogance
What is it makes us

Fling ourselves upstream
I was right up close
My fingers resting on his face
To the delicate regime of his jaw
Would you like to come in
For fifteen minutes

A carapace of entitlement
How shall I right myself
Let's stick to banal civilities
I repeat the words
He cannot bend towards her
We console ourselves

With repetition
She turned toward him with such eagerness
Such affection. Would you like to come in
Hope it's a wonderful day
For fifteen minutes
Happy birthday

CLEVELAND

Across the façade on every third frame were the stone faces

Of animals and inside, showy towers of apples, an extravagance of limes, a
　　cascade of orchids,

Flashing first then tumbling down, the solid weight of meats, bright pink
　　slabs of fish.

Reading and looking, we did not buy or eat. We did not always know the names.

To walk the streets or to tour your studio, we had agreed to pretend,

A blank brick wall lit by high windows, and in the middle distance through
　　bright pink air,

A view of a foundry, the flashing arteries of cars. What might you be planning
　　to keep.

And you turned away and turned back again to gesture towards a showy line
　　of monuments,

An extravagant granite fountain, or the elaborate plans for the public gardens
　　which I pored over

As if my memory depended on them, this improbable remembering

To which I had agreed. Until a sudden flash of feeling let me see

That there were train tracks all around the downtown and your empty studio

Looked out over seven bridges where they made occasion to celebrate your
　　comings and goings

As if they were only yours and yours to keep. As if you never meant to leave.

On the radio you spoke up and about your work

Always assuming an extravagant listener. In the middle distance.

The solid weight of a confidence that was not quite yours.

Not to be outdone, what you will keep. On every third frame, flashing first
　　then cascading down.

We did not buy or eat because we had agreed. And the ricochet of my coming
　　then going,

Or a card I had sent you, hung on a bright pink wall that was otherwise bare.

Ever or never, cut from its frame, on the granite slab with a paper cutter.

A sudden sleep I had in the quiet of the paper house while the next-door
veterans drank and sang.

And a valium tab that kept me from any memory of your comings and goings.

I bought a watch. I bought two watches. You sat on a bench

And thought about the rhetoric of monuments. Their bronze or stone faces.

And as I write, I am making a better language for this labyrinth.

This hermetic way of feeling. What might I keep. Flashing first, then
cascading down.

So at the battle monument, we walked round and round, reading and
looking at the names.

They were in the throes, the soldiers and sailors, some lining up or leaning
back or sighting out

The mute but puzzled faces of their enemies. Some now aiming just to flail
back and die,

Cast in green bronze. All one artist, and the human figures reel and march

And make their way, in a cascade around the towering obelisk, without
making any effort,

Without ever even moving, across their solid pink slab of granite,

With the convention center and the old hotel, and the civic plaza all
humming or flashing,

All looking on. Memory also reeling back or marching up.

Without the slightest effort, what I can make. From within the quiet of this
paper house.

You said, one shouldn't make things just because one had the space.

Or inside the frame. If any of my words might have lodged with you.

In the extravagant quiet, I could not keep. I could not say.

Later on I would walk to the gate, and then I would sit on a plane

Riding south through the bright pink air, the fuselage flashing and humming
through a cold

I could not yet feel. But until then I was walking down a street with you
Or pretending to walk and you took my hand or pretended to
As we studied the mute but puzzled faces of the animals
Which we had identified frame by frame.
Or the museum where I sat alone on a bench and watched a photograph
        of a field of snow
Fill slowly with flashing lights and the humming of a cello.
You ate a cup of soup. You answered your phone and then ended the call.
Looking off in the middle distance. What might you keep.
Through the cold bright air I did ride.
I cannot claim a mastery of this making, of the ricochet of memory, of the
        fixity of frames,
Without making any effort, without ever even moving,
Of the shocking weight against the slab of granite or of this sudden cascade
        of words
That began when a human figure tumbled out of the departing train.
Cannot claim your extravagant fingers or your sudden look away or the
        middle distance.
I cannot stay to say what else I cannot claim.
Had no claim. Who could ask for more.
In every third frame, the weight of an unnamed wanting,
Tumbling down from showy towers, to the bright pink slab,
To the strange quiet of the aftermath. Until you insisted on stating your claim.
You have made your peace with your own declensions, in a language flawed
        by a late beginning.
How much more might I have made, the heavy stone folds swung back to show
The mute and puzzled faces, or the curtains of the paper house swaying
        extravagantly,
Like memory, swaying in late summer like this methodical cascade,
The geese who know no other way but this tumbling southward propelled by
        the season

Or the flashing lights of the water below, now riding south through the
    cold pink air.
From within the quiet of this paper house, as if you had offered to
    "Place stamp here."
To "Tear here after folding." To "Press while turning." To tear away.
As if this was something like filling the frame.

U N T I T L E D

Margaret Butterfield

She

returns after long absence ,

though without memory   ,

scans the shoreline,   a form for waiting.

One dozen blood oranges in a blue bowl.

Running slant length of sand-spit beach

ten years after —herself ahead of herself—

as if having circled the world.

The distance she hopes to find is missing.

Good Friday spent bushwhacking a clearing by the creek.

Saturday, digging a garden.

Easter Sunday swimming at high tide.

The story:
     desire without object
     her skull sheathing her
     household Gnosticism.

Everyone knew a separate instance,

         taking their different yet predictable parts.

    Contingent upon a willingness to act.

    Awakened by small birds,

no, not awake;   asleep, still dreaming.

      Four—   yellowgreen—

no larger than hummingbirds but with short beaks, plump bodies.

      Heartbeat   ,   wingbeat   ,

      clung with tiny claws to ear's bow.

COHERE

We had occasion to dance.

Leapt

from boulder to reflection,

an indication
that entering any surface we become subject.

Trout taking refuge in shining,
rarified air

leapt

into our hands.

Fishtailing above
rivulets running flat over slant rock.

Fingers splinter granite
through fur or scales after crossing.

Sun-bowed crescents bent by pebbled riverbed;
       amber slice of light, coral shift of silt,
serpentine migration.

Waves a series of bright glances.

Four thin lines

               —claw-raked sand—

describe nocturnal forage.

She sits on the shore of a lake
within whose indigo dome
twin moons eclipse.

Stars punctuate ether
relieving dream's inordinate landscape.

Leaves and the shadows of leaves overwhelming green.

Ancient stories repeat.
How can she counter.

Letters carved in stone yield a callus.

He paints
      loopy, tangled vines,
      thin blue lines,
      a sea of semi-emergent figures.

Sailor, surfer,
whether landlocked or at sea,
riding wind, waves.

Sand or saline, kelp like fins
stir the strange current.

Violet underside viewed as solace.

Leaves burnt brown, yet iridescent.

Smoke spirals up
squeezing everything that breathes.

Am I flame or cinder,
will I burn or fly.

Whether white or transparent,

without words:
only light.

These talks serve to stir up waves where there is no wind,

How I prayed for rain and it rained for weeks.
Each new shoot in the garden
vigorous, erect.

Following light's sensible orbit—
to turn toward: tropic;
to turn from: misanthropic.

                    Working a raised bed,
hoe bent by buried rock,

shin torn because I swore.

                    Air rent by oath.

or gash a wound in a healthy skin.[1]

A serpent appears removed from
its distance.

It comes to disillusion, yet is surprised
by understanding.

A child adrift
waits.

The rocking sleep of water lilies
gives way to a horse and rider

who

wade through shallows
thick with cattails and bulrushes.

The rider inclines toward the child's face.

Shape a relation to that which emerges.

Terror and innocence alike withdrawn.

Face to face to become
what is asked before asking;
body a substance between that which is
surface or soluble.

Waiting for sleep, song, suitor, saint,

to lull the traveler allowing entrance to the future.

As if writing were a continuum that could be entered.

[1] *These talks serve to...* Master Mumon. Zen Comments on the Mumonkan.

ROOM THIRTEEN

Erica Carpenter

At the foot of the stairs one of us keeps talking.
It is apparent to all of us he does not know what
he is talking about, so when one of us sees fit
to cough, we all are coughing. Compulsively,
for sake of something, something's dry and
urgent plosives. Something fiery, hung like flour.

It's sounding dry and nervous like a mouse
behind the walls. Fretful but not frightening
is that cleave of lathe from plaster, and from
nearby rooms the sound of running water.
Water disports itself somewhere. Behind
some walls, presumably. Presumably all
down bird throats of pipes complete
with rings and tags and other markings
which, when drawn, communicate
pure passages of love.

, , ,

Someone concedes to going back against the issues
as if patient, as if clinging to a rope, a cause, a lifetime
copyright or patent, yet even now this one is picturing
a function of some spirit (he's the soul of generosity),
rising steam before his eyes. It's like a bowl.
A bowl of something. Yes, a bowl.

Now there follows a familiar slow collapse, surface waves
under surveillance of some close or passing storm. Reined in
again, he is the soul of forced contrition, and before his eyes
appears a certain parti-colored ball. It's a ball of a variety he's
seen, perhaps he's read about, before. In books it forms round
pools and near the ocean. Even he had such a ball, once.

, , ,

Neatly sectioned it its colors, like a grapefruit
in its skin, no, of course he'd never owned it. Someone
else had owned the pool, that is, the ball, or else it's
everyone that owned it. That is, it seemed so bitter
in those cold extremes of grass, and he thought
he saw the ball there like a floater. Like a floater,
as his dad was wont to say, something shifting
toward the eyes, the green, the golf course,
on the sea. A buoyant point beyond a pale
and thrifty pass, it kept emerging
out where nobody could find it.

What no one owns, he says (but always quiet,
sinking quick, more like a diction rendered fat
and soft it takes the breath away) *is mine.*
He begins to think of that domain so long
and yellow after fences as domain he "mayn't
be long gone to" (still imagines that such lyrics
might make sense, for once played out across
the blankets like a tiny civil war) – it reminds
him of his travels in St. Louis, in St. Croix.

, , ,

Of that obscure locale he can recall only one thing:
a bistro painting, rather odd, which seemed to cling above
a fault line on a bowstring plaster wall. A fin, an end
of something, it seemed ominous and dorsal. Its subject
was some animal resembling a – what? It was a walrus,
with the figment of a boot about the ears, tendered
heavenward in greasy blasts of blue. He bends
and sounds, suspects the bubbles in his person
like a faulty hand-blown glass, attributes them
to "battage," which is local, meaning something,
like the look that warns *bad soup.*

A word that sounds like what, crossed
with the memory of what he'd had for supper,
every night of life in that decayed October province
would conceal its lovely name, vague as clerks
who passed him numbers in the market.
Wagons passed him, he decided, every time
he closed his eyes. Otherwise it was the
avenues of houses moving westward,
below board. Hooks and grapples fastened
signage to the storefronts, and would likewise
tow his body through its complement of days.

And the ball beyond the pale, the dipper's bead
and prow. It was his luck to be that way disposed,
so that the fear of integers released him nightly
into ecstasies of looking, although sideways,
at the blanks between the stars.

SMALL BED DIARY

Valerie Coulton

1.

What deemed too heavy to carry left behind,
but these were our most valuables. Whites dirtied
easily find difficult to make clean again
but scarcity requires scrubbing. Hunger too
a catalogue of wishes: circle what you want and
wait for proper hour. Parts of you overweighted
with past desires. Skinny kittens skittering in the
courtyard, appetites non-metaphorical. The cook's
son's name is Agamemnon and he has locked up
all the wine

2.

Peering in, see nothing. Punctuated night,
necessities piled on little table by the bed.
Must be a woodman somewhere, should be
seen and not heard. Invisible, inaudible lengths
falling about his feet: what's he thinking
anyway? Orange ear protectors project from
memory. Oblivious we go, our noise is only
for the others. One bird calling for his
brother; the other one, a bit demented,
obsessed with the number eighteen

3.

Power saw and plate clatter: tapped keyboard,
kitchen voices. You are free to leave
by dreaming. Shuttered passenger, nose
outlined in waves of sleep. A man will
bring all machines you need to accomplish
your work. He will come by boat. Every machine
has its own box, its own
intention. If you don't know which to choose
try them each by each

4.

Apparent bird lives filled with grief
and terror: imitations make laughter after
dinner under stone arches. A mother's
pastichio, a son's enormous silhouette.
Conversation with belly always one-
sided, fear of fasting stapled
somewhere to the mind. Dry rice everywhere:
will we have to dance? Cross outlined in
blue lights. Your room is a box, a shell
already full of night

5.

Several trees selected to signal water
by sound of leaves:
here you will find a spring slightly muddy
and two German landowners with dog.
Sun's money falling everywhere from gateless
sky. The body is a vase you are forming
for your soul's return

6.

Missed spelling. Place requires name
as taught in bible school: Adam running here
and there, unsympathetic personage with
list of names. Arrive finding every thing
classified, rest by roadside to admire Monarch
butterfly, work of later namer: first these purple
flowers then those, with your wings
closed you approach invisibility

7.

You never know who you will meet: landscape
previously as windowscrap grows and
grows until the noblemen standing by that
square have disappeared, been forced out
of the painting by hills and cypresses and whatever
else. Outside the frame they pace in soft pointed
shoes, displaced, complaining, looking for the way
back in

8.

Lives of famous stones. The ones called nothing
and all with names cemented up and down
a mason's imagination. People have driven
up and walked into us expecting sights.
Nothing to see here but us at our condenseries:
red car, fennel, a few clouds on their
way to the sea

9.
Revise the grasses: ink insufficient to
burn again. Summer's work. September
ochre, where unhidden skin to redden by
midday glass. Someone has left a fish
in this stone. Man models boats, limps across
the courtyard. Were speaking of drunkenness,
were eating honey. Song without verbs. Dog,
sea, road, sky

10.
Unripe figs. Do you speak English? Build
table, feed dog. Subtract daily. Private
kindness, calibration of
waiting, habit to lock. If you had to forsake
a sense, which one would you choose?

11.
Reading the newspaper boat prior to its maiden
voyage: a foreign alphabet. Advertisements
mostly: can you laugh and swim? Single
pair of shoes subject to theft by dog mouth

12.
Having spent six years speaking wants to
speak again with prior chemical tongue.
Tongue also hanging out to lope along
a sea road shinily as chocolate. Would
never abandon smell, what about hearing?

13.

Displaced from familiar, find anxious
edges, precipice of speech, tight curves
in the road, falling worm, jointed insect.
Self intractable,
difficult, inert. To change must walk,
convince mind by shedding
salt, or curl shadewise facing mountain,
hidden from the sun

14.

How many kinds? Hours would not call
you, asleep under wood, under stone shingles.
Would pay for names of stone, of hours, for any
words didn't know. This is myth, but what isn't?
Now it's time to gallop down the gallery,
now to measure shadow. Every insect
is a clock unburied, about to take flight

15.

Inclined to associate crudeness with antiquity,
seers might be disappointed. Fish, carved rope,
orthodox cross. In one corner our computers. The
church is closed. Free to look at dog, to amble
in red shorts, to lend your idiom. Are we seeing
something here? Kitchen retrospective, dress
white as paper. Back in the
car, maps and plastic bottles. Bowl of water lined
with stones

16.

Left behind now abbreviations, bestiary, list of
beloved monsters very short and heroes even
shorter. River color of eyes hard to remember
but think all these colors were more or
less represented. Be unfooled by fire as
soft personages repopulate the roadscape.
Seek a clearing in the self where might
be of use

17.

If you ask him he will fly out again
unless mistaken for another. Someone teaches
you the little rules and makes a bracelet to remember.
Nothing for sale here, not even sound. Saying
a day is not a spell, just such lyric impulse.
Rejecting romantic in one self to cultivate an
other. This or that wing buzz, or a plane hung
in the last sky

18.

Involuntary soundtrack, oblivious fruit. Wood
slightly wet. Rely on devotion to clean
habit, those distant machines. Stuck paper
tears in your hands, you receive too many
messages

19.
Falling also good, remind to skin's frangible.
Artifacts of the body counted sinister, but
this is culture also as preferring not to
sleep in another's grave place. Clipping of
hair, fingerbone, small box of baby teeth.
Prefer people conservative with self,
liberal with other. Certain spirits change you by
reshaping your speech and the cast of your
eyes. Make awkward with others,
rend your own. Offer clipping, curl of
hair

20.
Disregarding center: guardian cypresses watch
over fish and serpent. A mistake in the budget
makes absence, paper to stone to paper
again. We believe in language and like it
rumpled, beloved old blanket. Behind the mountain
a real sea pushes clouds across the hour

21.
As though desiring discomfort but these are
only explanations: whether wild is not a question.
Puts every object into mouth except when
made to stop, this is studying.
Silent beside wall, more presences, it's
time to pollinate. Chew wax to remember
the time before this time

22.

Will give you a cream curing everything: now
no excuses. Modest blackberries, a house for
dog. One is a cat person, one has a
magic olive tree. Everything you need is
right here except milk: what happened to
our goat? Come to collect by side of road
munching berries and weed clot. What
is hard inside you will not give but
even stones conserve the sun

WE EMBRACE IMPRECISION
A SIDE-EFFECT OF DISTANCE

Caroline Crumpacker

There being no such thing as silence   only racket
          and no known calibration   for the elements needed
                    to make   it   disappear

we contrive   silence   as lack of attention   lack of speaking

We want   assurance   but from whom?
We want to know that   something will catch us   but what?

          What's Wrong with you?
          He said *Oh, nothing is wrong with you.*   we were at the edge
                    of language and disgust   and we were sweet
          not talking   not thinking   just vibrating
                    little waves of being   onto each other   . . .

The image of a net, cast off of a boat: white thick curling into the life-water   . . .
          and the reeling in.   Clutch of belly life sea life under-life.

if we give up   *this*   what will catch us?
          There is no such thing as freefall   but uncertainty is the same thing
          unless you train your mind.

He was   beautiful stumbling
          there is no such thing as intelligent nostalgia
but   I remember   that person
I invented as we walked upstairs
What are you wearing?   I stole things   and then I gave them back.

male silence reads as disdain   and female silence as erasure.

So to not be erased we talk   which is the erasure of our silence
          our imaginative self   talking whispering   noting   nothing.
Nothing is wrong with you?   Yes.

          there is an erasure which nothing will catch   .

The image of water   with no boats   one seamless horizon

with an underbelly of   riot.
                    ultra-sonic love songs.

There is no catching them   just knowing them.

Time   leans away from us   she is talking quickly nervously
          little nets thrown out   and ignored
I like her   but   I have nothing

our constant calamity   reads as no calamity
reads as nothing   the   aporia   :
the earth would not betray us   even as we betray it

nets   abandonettes

silence   audible   as a choice to stop listening
          inwardly   ...

A CHARM DETECTION

The impulse to   semiotic repetition   increases.
As we feel increasingly deceived.
Personal deception   is a position.
But social deception is a doctrine.

My daughter has   hysterical vulnerabilities.
But I have none   :

I undress   & the amplification of my disrobing is
       a violence.   I undress and still I am loaded with product.
       Mothers are a loading zone, yes   and yet as a mother
tethered to social meaning.
I don't refuse   .   I wear it and
at least a virtual body reaction like nakedness takes place   ...

When my mother died the world loosened.
As if falling off.   I felt the breeze where I had never felt it before.
      A space   not public, no, immensely private.

Consider her absence   as a vector
       a contract between us
        so many spaces that are both familiar and alienated
virtual sensation   is more addictive than actual sensation
       because it gives even less.

I have no cracks,   just dullness.   Like a rock.
My mother says when she is dying "You are a rock."

I love him tightens.
My child tightens.
My house tightens.

We are talking about our dead mothers.
A room full of us.
Talking about ourselves in light of dead mothers. In the light of dead mothers.

Yes   ethics matter more than doing.
My ethical ability has deformed around   my tactical ability.
My daughter spits the world out through her body.
I hold it for her. I am a rock.   She bathes in the sun on my surface.

Erin Mouré says: Admonish wit, at wit's end, where "wit" is.

I am at wit's end. And yet my wits go on. Without me. I stand waiting   for them
to release me but they give me form   without them I am the ether of social
meaning I have a man and a child and a job I am tethered to the narration you are
used to you can relax in my presence I am a rock.

     So that when the balloon is punctured you are no longer outside of it.

My wits contain me. My meaning.   Men are good
at ascribing meaning,   even if vandalized and indolent.
Look at me. I am a rock of love   and affect   .
I am naked as the bank and my wits abound   their end abounds.

I am directly perfectly   proportionally   aligned with their   endpoint.

FACT OR FICTION

The terrace is full of birds
and the coffee in its white cup
on the terrace is full of birds
or
is a container in which
the sight of birds   lands
as a lyrical impulse
meaning a strategy of image-making
rather than a series of occurrences.

Following the logic
in which the container is
held accountable   for its surface operations

great violence   is possible
          even   desired.

A philosophy
of tiny proportions

      meaning

There have not been congregations
      on that terrace
      for years.
The cup deludes itself.
And so forth.

This time the lyric is a moment of respite
but next time it will perform hallucinations
on young ladies.

The smaller ladies will sing aubades
The gentler ladies will sing French *lais*.
The perfect words for the perfect crime
              will oft be sung.

The verbal impulse
              dictates
that the birds remain a tool of allegory
and as such they are confined to hysteria.

The hysteria of their flight.
The hysteria of their oils.
The hysteria of their sexual activity.

The articulation of a thought,
              the perfect articulation of   a form of hysteria.

Meaning a long-abandoned porcelain
              cup   astride the day

       extends the thought.

Begin the operation again.
This terrace harbors a position
in the form of doors opening and shutting
            randomly but with lyric intensity.
That which is mine is strewn about
                the singing.

Mi amore:

This was once a place of congregation.
This was once a place of conjugation.
There was a banner unfurling in the wind.
Now it is the image
            of the banner unfurling in the wind.

We have called for the stillness
of the mirror as psychological trope.

We have committed false diagnostics
            and said *Oh. Let it be that still.*

AFTERNOON OF THE PUBLIC BODY

His meal pushed aside he speaks with deliberation
       implying   mutual satiation   rather than
     the force of appetite
        and yet she feels   mechanical
        a mutilation   of her uncanny goodness

the narration   locates her assumptions
     and puts the fever to them   by which I mean her body becomes aware
     of its choices   as a kind of death.

Staring at her photo   I say if you ever get bored
     I will stare at her for you.
     Love makes the crudest   propositions: devouring the object   ...

And yet the   long silken arms
     being in love as a political action
:
aestheticzed   inside the tiny leather valise
     a hoax a false back through which the female slides out

it is an art: staring at her picture   ...   *What is your favorite City?*
       city of secrets   the dead cities
    the way we talk about   habitation
    the naked woman in the public fountain
    ...   my favorite city   the filmic glory
  for a moment that reverie
    is the one we live in
    far from the one we belong to   the blank field

if you want me to stare at her
I will   I will devour her   my favorite city is the one in which
the man pushes the plate from his body   after swallowing
quivering delicacies   fresh caught
the children of the city are various and their work is gruelling
            as we wander deeper into the living quarters
            we realize   that   without them   it has no spine .

Love should refuse union
            the messy gash the mute cities the aspirational cities   ...

as the populace bathes sleeps   eats

a period of satiation may precede the use of force
even   that sparked between people

My favorite City is the one we consume
My favorite appetite is my satiation

Love   as an urgent   spasm of self
a plate of quivering proposition
all that has been attempted   is there with us within us
to keep force at bay   all that has been lost is there
to keep our hopelessness   from descending into   romantic tropes
            one body   ascertains   another as a kind of meaning-making
            and moves away   from its insistence   ...

RECHERCHE THEORY

The superheroes falter   expectedly
and yet   the trope of the avenger   frayed as it is
          is in vogue   .

A woman's thighs   network news.

Cheryl, the secretary   hijacked.

Why do I want to   and how many ways can this   idea be stolen
          before it is empty   and   the young life   within
          is dissembled   ravenously   ...

The woman with the two cars blocked in her yard   ...   and a drug habit:

You don't know her
and your aesthetic   doesn't know her.   And yet   the   similarities
          are revolting

This street   is rigged she   cries.

The newcomers   on their stoop   whispering.

The zoning board breezing by.
The parsimony of togetherness.   Neighborhood embrace thyself.

When she says my heart is not broken
          the momentum shifts   for all of us:
in our greedy pockets of sentiment

in our corrupted texts   out staggers
the need for physical coherence   …

Being cared for   is an implication   that
we don't live entirely on   the outer layer.

though drunk though medical bills   though debt   though historically

She screams at the passing cars "You must be crazy!"

SOURCE
: FAMILY

Susanne Dyckman

arranging, one can suppose,

a plate, bowl, water in a jar

simplicity, for others to enjoy

more action than story

daily service given

to first syllables

ma and *pa,*

though expelled

from the mouth

made kin

: S I S T E R

I can find *adelphos*

but not you

I discover what brings me closer —

it is in *sorrow*

and another, more to what I once learned meant *street*

concrete appearances

paved words lifted from the sediment

: H O M E

with little

room for _____

with little to be held

under a single roof

shared but separated

barely by walls, run down as rain runs

down to stain

then, *hold*

being a village where one rests, or lies

with many under one

as in the Irish   from *dear*

something near, cherished

but how,   to cherish such source

which is also the same as *end*, our long

and final purpose —   from *what one needs*

URGENCY OF THE CANYON

light is not haunting but ubiquitous
when you look at the sky
that is death
places of darkness turned
shimmering and luminescent

I begin the plea

to the good gutter   maybe there

the broken string of an impossible word

maybe there the glass Venetian rosary

to grind in my palms

everything illuminates

even fires

burnt out and sucked back

into the vortex of lightlessness

from the bottom

of the canyon

I track your

body

a figure

of five lucent points

yet with all the graces

essential to

white-winged rendering   your leap across

OMENS

Kelly Everding

A cow lows three times.
Rats leave a house.
A cat spits at midnight,
and a white bird
smashes against a window.
An owl brings tidings.
Furniture creaks without cause.
A church bell strikes
while the parson intones his text.
Children born under a comet.

The lost wax from a candle
is a shroud.
A picture falls from its hook.
Meeting a goat unexpectedly.
A shrew runs across your foot.
January—bad for kings.
A shark following a ship
is a sure sign.

A dead man
knows what is going on
until the last spade-full of earth
touches his grave.
It is dangerous to walk away
and leave a book open.

WITH EXES FOR EYES

She will bury in a hollow
her cold potato.
A boy with polio, up a tree,
watches, crutches hanging.
Her lids refuse
to close. Abandoned nails
at the door glisten,
a frozen rain driving through
an alien invasion of ions.
She will marry nails to the hollow,
sage tucked in her sleeve.
Already she drove nails
through the potato's eyes
all five, and hung a bell
for the blind. Children
follow, but hide behind trunks.
She will peel off her clothes—
her skin wound in ropes and rags,
her language a hook and worm.
She will sing children
from the shadows of oaks
and pluck their eyes.
She will give the potatoes their eyes.
The nails rain down.
The moon a hammer keeping them there.
She will replace each child
with a cold potato,
tucked into bed,

squirming under sheets and soiled,
its five eyes crying sharp tacks.
She will feed the children to the field
under watchful stars in a dead cold.
Her hair rises like questions.
Her fingers turn the soil
and return her words borrowed
for this occasion.
The ground restores the familiar bundles.

FONTANELLE

I handed back the baby
but no one knew
I kept the small, soft
back of its head
in my pocket
for a souvenir,
the space waiting
to harden.
I kept that
and nobody saw,
except maybe
the baby
staring coldly.

INFINITE GRANITE

My ears ring, a syringe of sound stuck in the lobe.
When I was young I dated a black man,
his smoky breath I couldn't place.
Thill skotul mensk—kissing
a red tongue and other, my infant niece
sees the stone I'm made of.
How thick. Thone mufom plent,
yes planet, everlasting native.
The junkie who made them call me,
I kelt, I floided
the mask, face down, can't fast food no more.
Ears ringing. And she found her father dead,
her lips sing, ligden motiral. I'm sorry
for being sorry, sore sordiden.
You licked the lips of women.
I killed plants. I moved too slowly
for them, increments of fever,
black other, thing story.
What carried me away layered me.
Playar fiskum yn creplos, kill, cry, kiss.
There was fear of never, fear inflated oblong.
I cannot move because I am so thick.
When was I ever worthy of your trust?
We're all here in the same place,
our glacially slow reactions
to bleth, mive, kife.

BELIEFS CONCERNING EGGS

The yolk cradled in atmosphere
surrounded by fragile firmament.
Beyond that a giant mouth.

Cneph, architect of the world, has an egg
coming out of his mouth. To dream
of an egg is lucky, foreshadows great fortune.

What hatched from it? A light?
From a toad's egg hatched a giant bat.
No, it goes like this:

At midnight, let the white drip from the shell
into a glass two thirds full of water.
Place your palm over the glass's rim and turn

upside down. The albumen will settle
into a shape. A ship? A tiny desk? An elephant?
It will foretell your future occupation.

Inside you eggs plummet like comets.
An omen for a beginning means
something else will end

and begin again.
The first man sprung from an egg
dropped by Tien from heaven.

What is hidden inside the egg?
Who is resplendent in his egg?

The sun complicated in a nest
of clouds breaks free unbeknownst
to itself, surprised by fecundity.

AVEC

The French have a word.
Every translator gets it wrong,
mistakenly attributes it to a certain
destination, a scent—almond for example.
I had a childhood friend whose skin
smelled of almonds.
In her hands was a small box
she carried with her always but never
let me look inside.
She would smile and run away
or just across the street,
holding the little box aloft.
I remember lots of whistling.
But we mustn't stray from the original
formula—the cosine dovetails the chute,
so to speak, establishes a soft reaction
like the belly of a satisfied hamster.
One must have an ear.
I would try to get close to my friend
without her knowing and listen hard
for some sound to escape, scratching.
But the box was always mute.
She too was mute. But she had eyes,
hadn't she? And hands!
The way she held the box
was a language all its own,
a language without a translator.
I made many attempts, drew diagrams
and numbered illustrations.
It was all speculation.
Her hair the color of light after a rain.

TECHNOLOGY OF DEAD VOICES

What he said was in my ears.
Sound so slow to leave.
A window curved on a bubble.
Played it. I can't see
the next room. There was no room.
A voice came from it.
His voice left his body.
I trace my finger along a path
that ends right here.
Hello,
he said. The voice unable
to reenter. His
voice stuck in the air.
Rewind.
He is slow to leave.
Every day a little more of him gone.
The sound of deep wood.
The sound of winter erasing.

THE WEATHER IN SPACE

We were speaking when the stars began:
a realist, you said, would consider them dead.

I wondered aloud what nebula
would call this a home—

children inching closer with sticks and shovels,
flagrant in their disregard of luminosity.

You said we inhabit a minor planet, and I thought
you meant music, my god you got the chord right.

Perplexed you spread your arms and said
The sun makes sweet poets,

despite the many suns snuffed tonight. Blink.
I mentioned an eminent meteor, or was it imminent?

It's nice by the fence, and I pose
for the satellite's camera, pinpoint light passing

through the Pleiades. You are on another
subject already, treason, and the wind

picks up, a treasonous wind relocating your words.
Select a chair, you said, when there were no chairs.

A dangerous transference, words thrown
from the mailbox—all stamped dangerous.
Do you believe in osmosis? you asked inching
closer, a coliseum blinking.

You say you're cold. In space meteors are mostly ice,
and you touch me your hands like ice.

I begin to see a pattern.
Look, the Big Dipper. We've seen it all our lives—

traveled that ancient path since we were amoebas.
Everyone has daughters bent to a loom,

weaving and unweaving, their stories a delay,
fortunes or doors. Don't change the subject.

It is nearly dawn and we wait for shadows.
Solar plumes lick the stratosphere, curl and blacken.

Inside the refrigerator
the light of a million concussions.
You have spared my feelings.
You are an azure plume, a drunken headstand
amid planet-wide catastrophe.
A jewel embedded with forests,
my train derailed to see the moon,
that marble.
Oxygen commingled with carbon that night.
Mysterious bruise arisen from what collision?
Get inside the room, your dorsal fin
submerged with fright when a hailstone
craters the walk out front.
The sky once empty now full,
the wind a hand slamming down its drink...
I have spared your feelings until now.
I am ink in your blue pool.
With every light on we
set the table mechanically—
you a spinning top, a blur of lines
gaining velocity, too bright, a double wattage.
My nose bleeds.
It is Friday before the end
in the note you tore from my hands.
The moon tears itself from the sky
with a prolonged shriek.
I see your organs working.
It is the day after and another reprieve.

MAN RIDING A BIRD

I feel the tines of the devil's fork
push into my flesh and the impending lions,
the wolf with a crane in its mouth.
Stones match stars in intensity.
An influx of cloaked strangers and scrolls
gripped by falcons, a river of liquid fire
with a voice like a canon.
I have read signs in the entrails,
black premonitions
spelled with coiled snakes.
But these are bits of shadow
emerging from light.

My children are bad investments,
my wife a regret with tears like knives.
I run toward a faded dream:
a wretched cart driven by headless dogs.
There is no knowing what will happen.
When the dead rise, who will house them?
Will their souls fit their sleeves?
What effluvium will leak from our ears?
My hand shakes. I go on with normal
things in my pockets.

SUMMER 1816, GENEVA

Renata Ewing

Woman-girl writing on the shores of a lake—

Drawn into secret
circle, the benefit
of an increasing moon.
A guitar with songs,
two poets "bumming
and humming;" two
sisters, sailing—
Glide across glassy
surface speeded along
by the wind. The boat's
tossing raises spirits,
inspires hilarity.
Majestic Mount
Blanc, the frowning
Jura. Splendid
notorious exile!
Happy as a new-fledged bird
trying its wings,
while village gossip
reaches English ears
back home. Stormy
weather, caught indoors:
"We will each write
a ghost story" to pass

the time. No thoughts
and then a waking
vision come to people
her terrible romance
waiting to be born.

MARGARET

Under water, first
hold your breath

Then learn to breathe
(the unknown)

Pockets, folds, crevices
conceive and grow within

Emerges in half dream
half waking

My swollen belly leads
irresistible urge

Forward despite
rules against temptation

Mountains between here and the source, thick forests—forgotten
all skills of navigation—attempt a landscape I cannot comprehend.
Pregnant, I carry a child in a crumpled paper bag—no grounding—
nothing save gravity holds my light limbs to Earth.

VICTOR (AT UNIVERSITY)

The World a secret that is mine to discover! I long for power, for glory, yes. But more, I long to relieve the suffering that is our collective fate. I was privileged to be born to parents who adored and supported me; I wanted for nothing. Then at 17, I watched my beloved mother wither and die in three days. From splendid health to wretched death in three short grueling days!

We allow death to rule us when we could rule death! My grief burns in me, but with its force and all my learning, I throw myself into my project. Like a hurricane, I will pursue Nature to her hiding places!

I've lost all soul and sensation, save for my pursuit—

CREATURE TO HIS BELOVED (NOT YET BORN)

Sweet Being, dearest dream, my gasp of breath
Be not mirage, be tangible, be!
These lips I shall press to every jagged seam

My clumsy fingers heal
Each rupture, each break of yellow
Sweet Being, dearest dream, my gasp of breath

I would not bring such misery
Except together we transform—
These lips I shall press to every jagged seam—

This hellish world to Paradise
Dwell in our first garden
Sweet being, dearest dream, my gasp of breath

The children of a god we together
Must name or invent
These lips I shall press to every jagged seam

Calla lilies shall adorn our rooms
Beside the sweet wisteria
Sweet Being, dearest dream, my gasp of breath
These lips I shall press to every jagged seam

ELIZABETH TO VICTOR
(MOMENTS BEFORE HER DEATH)

Husband,

I am devoured!
your devoted,

Written out of the story
given no choice

A bomb dropped on a city
wipes the slate clean

In the progress towards power
who is defeated?

Do not turn back, you cry
yet cry now as you hold me in your arms

Chronology reverses
only in dream

A step towards the future
embrace such nightmare

As if the bombings
Ended it

Why we did it! Not,
why did we do it?

Not question,
but answer

Scorched throats
of the people

Clamoring—

THE CROSSING

For days we've lingered on this painful shore.
Two camps formed: The living, the one who'll die,
cling for time against silent water's roar.

Old friends and new gather to say goodbye,
meet eyes grown huge, clutch frail hands, kiss pale face,
leave for the world again stammering, *why?*

For months we've journeyed to this last embrace:
It's not from lack of love that we betray—
implacable force leads us to displace

you as *other*—as we whisper and stay
at bedside beck and call. Alone at core
you're left to navigate swift river's sway

forge a path through the silent water's roar.
For days we've lingered on this painful shore.

U . T .

Your mother in heaven sees when you're bad,
teacher warned (she'd known his mom, Mary Grace).
I never misbehaved again! My dad
claims with a mock cringe of fear on his face.
Until Knoxville, my father was devout.
Sophomore year Philosophy Club proved key:
Darwin reformed the saintly Eagle Scout.
From *repression* and *lies* set himself free.
Behaved then like he had nothing to lose:
Lost Christ in favor of evolution;
tossed from R.O.T.C. for his war views;
soon he embraced Marxist revolution!
    Convinced he'd been taught to believe in lies,
    the world would never be right in his eyes.

AT KAISER

Another trip to the oncologist:
Robert climbs slowly onto the table.
His blood pressure is too high from the stress
of the visit, his long limbs unstable.
We're here for the results of his CAT scan.
Tremblingly, he unbuttons his top shirt
reveals a green jersey, his face deadpan.
"Atheists" is scrawled on top, an overt
corruption of the local baseball team.
We cheer, he smiles, relieved by the humor.
Dr. Gordon arrives (whom we esteem)
and reports the progress of the tumor.

   In three months its size has nearly doubled.
   We leave Kaiser for tea, feeling troubled.

NEW YEAR 2007

Undetected he slipped back to white wine.
But when the malignant nodule lurking
like an alien egg beneath his skin
was found, he launched into full-time boozing.
Vicodin assuages the physical
hurt but only cheap white wine may suffice
for the passionate accumulations
of a long, varied, almost broken life.
And quiet fact of piecemeal destruction
as cells metastasize then lie in wait,
offer gleam of tantalizing reprieve,
before enacting their final checkmate.
 By birth we commit to certain endgame;
 What strategy prepares us for the pain?

MAPS

Do you dream about maps? My dad inquires.
No, do you? I'm rubbing his feet, *Why yes!*
His voice is clear, lucid, almost inspired
after a day of muddled consciousness.
I'm content to plunge into a terrain,
follow trails without benefit from maps.
While he'd sit, study contour lines, attain
insight for a new geography, hap-
py to remain home. Now that he's dying
he's scrutinizing a route for escape:
I just want to get out of here and cry.
No key illuminates, provides respite.
    Flesh vanished to bone he's become all eyes—
    Like a baby's—you see his eyes are wise.

PROLOGUE TO ILLUMINATION

Amanda Field

To make the bed is a ritual
surrender to daylight,
the uncomfortable habit
of shifting. Each day I wait
for the obvious to recede.
In darkness, love gets ratified,
an amendment, the song
I like to sit around and wait for.
But this is not singing, love
unbidden, bearing through.

MY COUSIN'S WEDDING

Bridesmaids twirled to a tank of music

while groomsmen fingered rifles in the garage.

The newlyweds were off somewhere

and there was only this lingering with the potato salad,

this getting born in the dark.

Morning arrived in the chemise of dawn

breaking and entering on the beige carpet.

Next door the box springs wouldn't stop clattering.

WINTER LANDSCAPE

The mud's a little theater
for sky. We live together
so our terror may recede
at the very least between
each other. What I loved
was you breathing next
to me and out the window
black pines like minarets.

WINTER LANDSCAPE

The mud is
these days
we live
between
what I loved

IN THE CITY OF LOST PERFECTION

Chaos ignites temperaments.
Charge out each day and plunder.

Bones be buried. Bones be broken.
Renounce blood, a larger black.

Each morning renew chaste vows,
only to unbridle by afternoon.

The way an ox would plow a field
drunk youngsters prove their anger.

A cadence of steel coffins hidden
by the king, a dispatch of flame.

Votive materials line cisterns,
a row of animal knucklebones.

Classical etymologies persist.
The holy and literal correspond.

Settlement embraces the fortress.
The darkest place is between two epochs.

Slowly closes the original circuit.
An endless feud signals stubborn days.

SHELTERING

I have not made the pilgrimage from this hour

to the location of mercy. Ashamed for not feeling

the golden touch, defeat spices the bones.

A neighbor practices the tuba.

A dog barks from her predicament in the yard.

Six days of creation wait on one day of abstraction.

The contents of my mind furnish the room.

When I lose myself to reason, seasons flatten.

YESTERCIDE

The body has been taken, yours

replaced by a chamber, red

sun through eyelids, evening

attached to day by a cord

more like captions than music

disclosing hunger everywhere

wider than dinner, rooms

with bright centers, empty.

MY MOTHER THE INTERIOR DECORATOR

She wanted nothing
more than for the house
to speak abundance,
the pantry replete
with bins of oats,
mercurial solvents
underneath the sink.

But that afternoon
an argument prevailed
against the blossoming
refrain of spring,
even while the house
reiterated its familiar
syntax of furniture.

PUPIL

Kate Greenstreet

A genius! they say.
Or then: She has almost no gifts.
Get the pipe in, and bury it.
What we began
to know, we began to know
in secret.
If you are vulnerable
to this music—

it's not about ecstasy,
merging, or being unusual,
believe me.
What we've done so far
is like assembling ingredients is
to hunger. If you are vulnerable.
(A great place to live!
In loving memory)
We thought the future

had arrived.
Fields,
a stony place, then forest.
All positions being apparent,
no one agrees about
what happened next.
It was the past. (*Shoe*
that fits)
Mathematics
was a prayer they did
with chalk.

I pondered the meaning
of the letters—thx (lowercase,
period)—instead of thanks.
Decided I had said too much. I waited
to be asked. Shoe that fits,
shoe made of glass.
Begins to explain
how in prayer
the soul is united with God.
Describes how we may know we are not
mistaken about this.

2 OF SWORDS

There's always that moment
with people, right?
You look back...
you can't believe

how they just
don't love you.
And how,
in the minute before that,
you didn't know.

There was a place, near water.
The people had come
from somewhere else, and settled.
How we came to exist.
How we came to be here, everywhere
at once.

How could I say nothing?

Well, it's a long walk ahead.
For a long time,
I didn't know.
And it's all just another
story about how life could be.

A psychic told me once I had the mind of a nun.
As if there would be only one kind, for nuns.
The offices of seers we consulted in the South
sometimes had chickens. The vestibules

were swimming with the poor—
bobbing, drowning, in our lake
of dreams and wishes.
Tell me everything
you want to do while there's still time.
Keep in touch.

Think about the leaves
and the birds
in branches.
Think about the words
Big Picture.
The Big Picture.

For a long time,
I didn't know what to say.
And of course I didn't want to say it.
When everything depends—has always
depended on acting like nothing is wrong.

Fruit trees blooming in the blood-drenched ground,
a ringing phone—
it's what we're in the middle of.

If we realized the extent to which no one understands
what anybody else really means
by anything they say, well,
you say we'd all go crazy.
But aren't we crazy already?
With trying and pretending and
being mad about it—I mean angry.

There was a place, near water.
How we all came to be,
everywhere
at once.

My prayer is changing.

9 p.m. on a Tuesday, the laundromat's closed. The last warm night of October. A few crickets. The last ferry comes in, so slowly. The fortuneteller climbs up a ladder with a roller in her hand, in a hot pink shirt. She seems young to know so much. She's been painting the inside of her place bright white. The door is open. The outside of the storefront they did last week: a surprising golden ochre. The streets are dark. One open restaurant, empty. Ropes slapping hollow metal masts, occasionally. Not much wind.

What's the appeal of a mystery? Someone is looking for something, actively.

THIS IS A TRAVELING SONG

The escaped convict's story is a traveling story.
The language is full of gaps and problems of tense.
One time you asked for a sign and found a shell.
Add one minute for every thousand miles.

We learn to speak by hearing sounds
and deciding what they mean.
My father was alive
but he was tired.
Sensitive to distances, the dangers
of spring. Guessing
what lies beneath the ground.

What moves below the ground
What stirs
under the ground
Guessing
about weather
Imagining the rooms

Some days, finding glass,
mostly green—blue is rare.
Add another minute.
Do they know we're here?

Learn the lesson of the pioneer.
Learn by losing.
Everybody's trying to get home.

We waited for the optimum conditions,
but in the end we set off in a storm.

DUSTING FOR PRINTS

The subject is distant from and dark.
The subject is seen through glass.
The subject reflects, or has a luminous body.

If you feel you can no longer pray, care less, don't be selfish.

Was he an artist?
I remember him cutting a sword out of wood, and painting it gold.
"Arms" seems wrong. It's their nearness.

Sometimes it's you and I'm calling to you but I say the wrong name.

Several glass ashtrays, the panther lamp. The light
bent toward the map. I spent a long time under the table, learning
to recognize wires. How we would change her.

How the bullet is scraped as it moves through the barrel.

The subject is distant, and dark.
Each instance has its rewards. Sex can't explain it.
"Their goal is to empty themselves."

If you feel you can no longer pray, personally, I like trees, birds.

Personal & unintelligible, my addiction bores me.
We still need spoons, plates, and knives. Bowls. Your star sign.
Those weeks with you?

I remember driving you somewhere. Driving, and it was snowy.
Nothing was figured out.
You said redemption looked like a painting of fire, after a fire.

DIPLOMACY

Start with a word.
The proper
name, the letter E.

tens of thousands
take a stick
you must expect to suffer

Think of the miners.

hooded people on the move
things keep flying or falling down there
you still hear about them sometimes
trapped

The eternal city

the wet ink
at the heart of faith

aged
and stitched
Or paved, for ease of use

They have a word
for it: "with new water."

Keep anger—his magnificence, certainly.

(I worry about
ice, if we get it wrong.)

They have a word for:
"without the shedding of blood."
Imagine anybody trying to boss me.

There's always someone
shouting up the stairwell
sick with the news
no keys

And if it's the father
coming back drunk

coughing up some black stuff from a hundred years ago,
it's okay

to be disappointed.

It provides some extra
space (the half life).
To dig a hole they used the antlers of deer.

The "E" on its back, burning
rocks in the cart, feet chipped.
Everything by hand.

No one likes this story so I'll get to the point.
(but what's the word?
think of something nice)

You read about people who have something else.

There's a wild donkey loose in the street.
All the dogs came out to the curb and stood together. Quiet.
Not moving, not barking.

BEING FOLLOWED

Years passed.
I looked back to see.

Answer the following questions with yes
or no or no one knows.

I had a small and frightening pain.
Aunt Patty called, in love with another dead guy.

Wrong number.
I regret our
bus routes
Our hidden drawer
Our off in the fog on foot

There were all these choices, these different *kinds*
of people. Who to kill, and
who not to kill.

the welders
the burners
Seeing the pictures behind the pictures.

Civil war
Ghost
Leopard
In my heart, I'm free.
But it's so secret.

DISAPPEARING INK

It's quiet lately at the fortuneteller's.
To control content, use actions.

"X"—someone who
hasn't appeared yet, but

whose purpose we deduce.
I know it's there.
Love, I think.
Or maybe it was goodness.

So many hopes for the outside.
(O hunger, O equivalent)

I approach it calmly.
It spills into everything.

Anne Heide

Finger stuck in the sky   if there is nothing for me here

to capture, there is nothing   for me here.

The brightest tree   was made of only oil

　　　called out my names

　　　　　　　　　　　　to the swamped up water.

　　　　　　　　　　　　Wood-colored water.

It's still alive if you can see it.

A bluette caught under my hands. Hands spread out like a feather.

And now the animals

on fire

fur, sit to warm themselves

in a trick of light

or glad stance

over the embers

Be *an enclosure.* Be *perchless*

Dear

I'd write.

To find in the fable

            I'd left you   ahome.

I have   beasts

        to find

                               my home

in skillful approach.

     Portions I'd saved for you   of animals

in my trunk packed up with blankets.

A mobile bloom   out of the mouth

comes   brightly.   A nattling at the window,

            crease the way of your palm.   Create

        the logic   of chance through   which

one locust becomes   another.

                    A bloom   pours

out of the sound   I'd spoken.

A little tragedy.   A fringe on the end of it.

An upright   recognition.

A reconcilable splitting, closing back in duplicate.

feb. 2

I've eaten a bit of you how the

bellow you make is all swallowed

up in my thumbs.

Who is trying to clip out the cloth

from my clothes. Who is trying

to peek out under my seized fist. I

look and you're a vanishing point,

a matter so dense I can't see.

SEA CAT

Milk comes from bone.

It holds its hands to the

white-wet green

so it can grasp whole

the whole slippery

moss. I don't give

it anything

anymore it has betrayed me

by making a sort of perpetual bowl

of its belly, sore and sweet.

mar. 12

Recognize in this mutiny: I still

dredge from the perfect pulse.

The thump that comes from under me.

A familiar. My head fills against

the ground: I wake you across the

shore by my listening. I am a

beast of too roused water. I am

set down here on land definite.

They say.

FOGSTAG

So with what can I stitch apart

the floored forest—forget.

Grant me a way to fall out of the granite husk,

so nothing's left straggling

through the mulch but me.

HARELIPPED

The hare loves the deer as much. Slips

unnoticed beneath her feet. Paws

her hooves. Slip and mortar. Thirsty water.

Who'd been chased: loved. White fawning

over her. The liquid offspring: hatch.

may.19

Have you ever heard such a labor

forth from my two fingers. A

pinch that regards a pain which

beads it, births it. Makes a round

amazement from my arced hand,

close enough. And suddenly, a

smaller beast of me.

N O . 4

Brydie McPherson Kiuchi

And it suffers yourself on the light
leaving day to the pain-bed:
so day in distrust is severe manner,
the quantity now open,
the crowds open up their momentum
on the mouths now,
traveling.

Words catch the air and leave us out,
though we want to be suggested,
to be in.

If salt is needed reaching is possible
trying to compensate crawling the lap,
why criterion if not inclusive, if not sentimental.

I, the Argus,
becoming effects on people,
bees under pillow for days in a row.

With misconception in view,
as any sort so popular would naturally be sorting these
snapshots,
becoming inaudible sand-deep,
the should-be-manageable plural.

Awake under moths in the road,
accurately reflect me outside.

A secret home might have calm voices,
holes standing in for windows,
asleep in a bed with shoes on, less breathing.
Chrome room, under the perfect tree.

And either they might
feel lucky and still not return.

And who desperate, all mine,
you have your aim, your arm over my neck.

Decide how to sit
at the same time this is happening, ageless bodies,
bounteous air-thrift,
vibrant busybody,
with flag décor
at gas station cutouts,
glimmering hubcap
stopped with the news.

If only blank looking were just.

To render our stutter has been my aim.
It would have been easy, and not useless,
but words are already bulky
and one has simplicity's merit;
before leaving having
dry hands through the metal detector
to get there
the two already first,
separate.

Embarrassed
to be there
with no fever.
What sounded like one imagines bombs,
there were still natural occurrences;
for instance, the meter maid issues us tickets.
On the thought-aged
led the run.
Unopened room
in which time
had meant order.

Home suddenly had arrived
had absorbed,
so much plum-in-mouth
having newborn.

At the time being hopelessly able.
In fact, enormous, so clearly passionate.
Fire at the height of a heavy night unplayed.
The repeatedly invoked.

Let's expect dead birds,
warm strips,
stable org-

Let's form a circle and run to the other side of the grass,
fetch the screen in the forest, beating a lung out.
In my own thighs, shiny oppositeness,
to the right "public," to the left real people exhausted.

The function of even thinking,
more cavalier,
one step closer to becoming vital.

Meant to bunt consciousness,
seeing in
trite little phrase.

(Little by
hardly understood parts   what's seen all at once
the performance aspect of it
faking it on the ladder, uneventfully,
we go shopping, shave grass, just to keep getting along).

Bound
amidst havoc
filial
to object
judging overtones as somewhat good and desirable
summer,
towards myself are suspect
to fall in my own lodgings, but being so fearful.

This, backed up by observation,
a warning put up with
to know in practice
what died in the hand.
Place, too, will take some
cruelty, some face value,
severe blow, one further point, being still more
lonely, admirable and probably guilt admirable.

Believing your archive now, the photos, the bystanders.

Drafts the fragrance of grass.
A flimsy disk of the land, one grated, some flung
at white rooms to the feet; and women swayed on
in other grim patches, but so bearable
and slight that leaves with deep grooves
sprung charged.

To blur while others sit legibly,
carrying limit.

Borderline slopes retrace each other and blush; paper seized from the jar.
One can bathe in clear water, perhaps more casual.
Are they somewhat better, found backdrops, walks, forced leisure.

The freeway trooped and ragged, conservative as a bend of field; a feather
turns from the light made moving this way.

erica lewis

lay all the edges together :: you don't know where the excess will be
in that nothing at all beside the piles sometimes i swim with you
in that ocean-sized room forced to hold on with our feet we fasten
no more to loyalty because we lived there once and were never at home
if you are honest you know the question and the answer yes we will
find other places and other people to care for us but you need to live
with the question

the concept of letting go in various forms :: i am adding to the smoke all this emotion broken into if i close my eyes pour this over this something in the corner of the room shifts and we understand it to mean ghost i thought you meant someone had nailed you down to one of your cares again but maybe it is the light outside and i am very excited by this time of year the devolving bits and pieces the voices you hear the coming together and falling apart of things the thing is that we all eventually fall apart but at least i know how i feel about facing my own weaknesses the shadows on the ground grow smaller and smaller :: you unapologetically wear the things on your chest i would have swallowed the entire ocean to get to the bottom of it but i am silent now and just hover over the things these partial happenings the little bit of grey between them the window was down and sand blew into my eyes but i was the electricity i was always the electricity i think of life after the wound heals :: i am wondering if this takes away from the power of we as zigzag lines some moment inside the flutter maybe it is a hair then that separates skyward as excess baggage i used to catalogue the words in my head like birds like you thought of the years i think about you all the time as a man who walked by but if it's up to me you never did learn how to want

the dirty projectors progress in spirals

a clearing in the throat
silences the sparklers and kazoos

you played it right
in a wave from the tower

i tried to think about it harder for a while
there is something about that song that gets to me every time

memory stands up in slow motion
repeating itself between the folds

i panic my little panic
though i've barely scratched the surface

nothing has changed here except the furniture and the weather

i felt it then the same way i feel it now
walking on the edge of things exhaling
pictures and pieces of glass into my palms
the noise of other people coming

the knowledge that
when i heard you live it was all lost on me

to begin the forgetting

we pass through this world with our surroundings

but we only learn one way

the dirty projectors progress in spirals

you can't see your future when you're twenty years old
we have our suspicions
but this isn't how it's supposed to go

fighting with the actual memory of things

in the wayward logic of a poem

it is mature some might say to realize things are so
but i've seen the circus i know how they do it

sitting on the sidewalk drawing pictures
with pastel colored chalk the shades of pink yellow and green
in the sunlight like neon

the cement slanting at an angle so that it feels
as if you could fall into it

into the correspondence of the position in which

life is elsewhere or dumbly passing by

all wax and feathers

you don't know what it's like
to sit and watch people wear their weaknesses

i sat down

for a.l.

the dirty projectors progress in spirals

it's hard to feel so i feel everything

when you wake up staring into nothing
you think about your destination all the time

the passage of air through the mouth
the name of some town or highway
whispering back and forth

like white noise
our eyes prefer purpose
and time does not finish a poem

so how could i have thought of this place as a reservoir
a place is not a reservoir i'm still the same person
running down the street

literally living down the pathology of trying
to recover something that probably never really existed
in the first place

i just want to hear something that's lasting and honest
i just want all the colors to be real

but i loved those polaroids
there should just be a whole book of those
things that hold people together that are not love

i know the meanings are more from my memories
but they never moved

what i mean to say is you are exactly where you are supposed to be

i think about you all the time

architecture is not about words :: it's about tears
your youth as a salt wound that ceases shape we go
by taste and touch and there are those you will find
only to lose again in images that pretend to be empty
and easy but are not sometimes it's just hard for us to
see when what we see is always distorted and what we
say inevitably falls short of what we mean i mean we
build ourselves from the drums up i see you sometimes
on the street standing there in the surrounding light
only so much smaller than i remember

the way we occupy our bodies :: our hard and fast rules
my anguished vocals constructing ghosts in an open dusk
you say it's romantic but the thing that makes me cry is
each time i say to myself it's just a poem no you don't live
here i live here and for the fiftieth time this morning i get
a lump in my throat because you seem basically happy
it's like when someone is in crisis and you can't do
anything but stand in the middle of the room waving your
arms and wailing we watch ourselves float past almost
in spite of ourselves how the waves track you down
the lightning strikes and we almost die

geography is a starting point :: so much so the sentiment makes me bleed when i was younger and you were younger we looked at each other the same way although i can't remember where or when it's not at all good when your feelings are so palpable but everyone my age has become good at performing when really it's about loneliness the shudder in your lungs when reality just doesn't feel "real" i found that year so painful and humiliating it becomes less clear to me now the further i get from it what was real and what was fake all of those emotions bleached to the point of abstraction like a sea of bees sometimes i swim with you in that ocean but you never have the urge to rescue the forgotten things

A DRESS FOR WEATHER

Susan Manchester

She wears only bird clothing   cormorant wings

stitch patch to patch   green quill work of skins

    s k y   s h a p e s   i n t o   w i n g s

           a   d r e s s   f o r   w e a t h e r

eye-thread of bone-needle   stitch it all

supple with seal sinew   tie shell-bit bead-bit

bone her sleeveless robe tied to serpent-bird

bird-bird bird-serpent for diving and fishing

where they fish stitching a cloak of tethered wings

reflected-iridescent   each wing in the cloud

work of weather

B'S RED BOAT

Whose flesh my lineal descendent?

Patterns branching

    the pith and width of bone

our cambrian green stems

    & calcified pockets

        worn seeds to gall wasp says:

            no one

            thing

            Begin in the water's deeps

      tidal rockings

   diatoms of algae bloom   slimy prisms

   cell pulse of swamp ooze

      sunlight orbits an egg

        spirals, blood rivulets

 life's sap soup

each

body falling

into cloud-furled larvae

Zona pellucida

swarm be moving

wired zygote, little harbor

our cells in embryonic swirls

tissue portholes of star particles

navigable coils of light

negotiable us

light pockets in amniotic nets.

Fluid &

fish scales

bridge in a bat's wing

mansions spread by amber sap

sea stack, this swell-smacked circumference , which—

which amphibian ladder

or aviary

what skeletal galaxies wash underfoot?

A human swimmer glides through water

kelp drift anchor for air   sees

horizon

surf alighted & salt blind

b's red boat

slips

into slow tide.

LONE WOMAN

What is lost

she catches in echoes of others

from beak openings she gathers shapes of speech

echoes: calls & whistles   *gull   guillemot*

plover & cliff swallow

                                        calling others

mouths wind off waves, slow sibilance of cliffs

in oak leaf language   cached in edges

speak to where the echo is—

                                        open

standing in the sand   warbles work the body

seal   wave   kelp   shore

shallows sound inside the bird

she lips   waterbeads

stitches into the veins of leaves and leaves on branches

and acorn openings of things
                               all sewn together

in sound around the island ear

                in its pinnae of wind

CERULEAN

Blue a deep greenish blue which is darker and deeper than pthalo

bluer than the ocean's horizon line of rain, more green

than a phosphorescent fish tail dropping toward midnight

a lithic cave light, green on raft bladders of kelp forests

and in the shadows, dark marine blue of a leviathan dive

DARKNESS SPITS THE AIR

Cloud wrapped lagoons and sea strewn waves

pitches   kelp   wrack   onto   rocks

islet

    augury

of salt etchings

                     bleached or buried or burned

                          the sea casts out—

a   wild bees' larva   maimed in   some way

MIDDENPILE #47
QUADRENT #2
SOUTH SHORE SANTA CRUZ ISLAND

ancient middenpile of
    communal fires
        where sea

saturates ash
    and domes of abalone
        broken glints

from the ground
    this midden mosaic
    constellates

clamshell
    charcoal
        skeletal fragments of fish

chert
    shinbone
        bowlshard &

mesh
    and lost
        olivella money-beads

all these Chumash

scatterings

now

thousand-year old

compost for

coreopsis

SHE WALKS

Floating among tide pools   lavic stir pots
in surf whorls of miniature life forms: eels
anemone urchin moon-like nacreous sheen
within the weft of weeds   she walks

walks   over billowing dunes and is pulled
into a gravity of grasses the tide's fringe
shadow of sands   where her village whistles
                                        wind-buried.

INNER MISSION

Linda Norton

This is a funny way to infiltrate a heart
       Little termite, you bore your way in

First you soften the wood with tears
       Then you go to work

Work ethic or no,
       you will do damage
              so incremental

       it's devotional

, , ,

Music about music can be music
as inner tubing can be sublime
at the right moment on a river
the color of a tire

, , ,

The wind came up the other day
      and tore some leaves out of a tree

At the same time a flock of leaf-sized birds
      flew into the branches

, , ,

We want our trees to topple in a storm
If they sink into the ground instead,
      morphing like something in Ovid,
        our hearts ossify

, , ,

The tree falls and blocks the road
We recognize this wreckage
        awesome nuisance

We can't get where we want to go
      and it's a comfort to know why

And nothing's wasted
We can use the firewood
      as we use a body at a wake

THE PUBLIC GARDENS

Get wisdom! Get understanding!
Do not turn away from the words
of my mouth.
                    Proverbs, 4:05

Not knowing any better
I took it for a blade of grass
and walked into poetry
in search of a place to rest,
a place to suffer formally,
a glade.

Now I am bleeding,
my mouth especially.

I cry out to tourists entering the gardens
with cameras and guidebooks,
shields and blinders:
"See how beautiful it is to suffer!
Look, I have become a rose!"

BRIGHTON BEACH

The old yogurt in the Russian bakery
The cat's whisker in my sherry
The cherry pastries
The man in the same place for a long time
Ravenous seagulls
The Mandarin oranges, six for a dollar, the leaves still on the stems
Russian erotica, a plump woman with big arms embracing an enormous man
The runner who took a tumble on the boardwalk
The noise he made when his knees and knuckles hit the planks
The man scooping lots of small cucumbers into a bag
His pickling plans in mind
The woman at the bagel place—her beautiful lips, fortitude, disgust, resignation
The old customer who squeezed all the bagels before he paid for them
The buttermilk we drank near the beach
The streaks of light on the water
The ship that looked like a city on the horizon
A Jerusalem of smoke stacks and turrets, disappearing
You, with rough cheeks
Walking close to the water, climbing the rocks
I recognize you by the shape of your legs
Watching you from far away
Where I sit near a Russian family of four,
Including a girl with enormous ears
And a toy passport

CALIFORNIA

Lyric & burden for freight train, harmonica, & peacock

The mind catapults a poem into the future
Girls pulse with the urge to deliver
Yarrow and oleander line the roads of the state
The crushed contraltos move back east

Here's a creamy transparency, a filmy depth
The boxcars make a nice apocalyptic sound
What does it mean when peacocks scream?
Who told you that you were naked?

Upholstery cracks in the noonday sun
Too soon new lipstick tastes of attic
A louvered cattle car rumbles to slaughter
A box of meat, a box of metaphysics

This day like others is entirely fugacious
Men die making gasoline for yachts and trucks
Blood and starch go together on a plate
The freight train slices the fat pink distance

GOODNESS AND MERCY

After we gave up, you put a record on.
Django Reinhardt played hard
on the other side of the room.
You started to snore.

An hour into it
a sideman shouted
"Play it!"
and woke you up.

We laughed.
Why did he call out just then?

Was it a photoflash
that triggered it?
A woman across the room?
A flicker of a psalm?

Yea, he was playing
in the valley of death
in a smoke-filled club in Paris,
and he was not afraid.

MISCELLANEOUS OPALESCENCE

I am like a pelican in the wilderness, I am like an owl in the desert.
I lie awake, and am like a sparrow on a housetop.

Psalm 102

And I am like a tombstone with a lark etched where a cross should be, like a book that has been read to death, like a tumbler at the back of a kitchen cabinet, the last of a set.

In the public gardens, in the fens and in the graveyards, shards of glass and pottery, billiard and piano keys, bones and insurance policies have begun to surface, as if New England were trying to speak of plunder, and of "the suffering that accompanied ivory."

But "after great pain / a formal feeling comes / the nerves sit ceremonious / like tombs," et cetera. Tombs with snow piled on top, and a crust of grit on top of that. In Boston the cemeteries come right up against the highways to vacationland. The enormous Catholic cemeteries, that is, where thousands of immigrants from Ireland and Italy are buried.

Vast grid of death, no arabesques or grottoes, all of the lanes named after the saints, and plastic flowers covered in snow propped on the headstones of the Italians. Nothing Gnostic or ecumenical here, no *God is Love,* no doves. *To Jesus Through Mary* is an insinuation when encountered here among the rows of granite slabs.

A lady in the front office near the gates smokes a cigarette and flicks through the card file with a dirty lacquered fingernail: "Mary Sullivan, Mary Sullivan, Mary Sullivan"—there are hundreds of them, cause of death listed in each case. Servants and mothers, bodies and souls, defiant girls with secrets hiding among them.

She sends me out into the snow with a map, and I forage among the Marys, and I am like a daughter looking for an answer from someone who can never tell. I am a daughter of loss and shame, of defiance, laughter, and a dream of glamour. And my Mary is like an opalescent jar on a windowsill at night—you can't see if she's empty or full.

Heraclitus, from *Cosmic Fragments*: "If all existing things were to become smoke, the nostrils would distinguish them." I smell the blood and smoke in the snow and ice, and I distinguish among all the Marys, and I lay down in the snow.

"For the universe has three children," Emerson wrote, "Jove, Pluto, Neptune . . . or theologically, the Father, the Spirit, and the Son." And one Mother, all Marys.

Across town in another season I wandered in a cemetery like an orchard or a garden, or a book, where New England divines and beneficiaries of the slave trade and abolitionists are buried among Yankees who warned of hordes of papists.

"Went yesterday to Cambridge and spent most of the day at Mount Auburn," Emerson wrote in his journals on April 11, 1834. "I forsook the tombs and found a sunny hollow . . . I heeded no more what minute or hour Massachusetts clocks might indicate."

I walked among the Cabots and the Lodges and stopped at the grave of the botanist Asa Gray, and the yellow leaves fell upon my shoulders as if I were an heir to something. An arboretum, a library, a porch, a problem. A trellis covered with vines of Concord grape. "She does not leave another to baptize her, but baptizes herself."

Tombstones are the covers of books, and there is no rare air, just blood and smoke and a library of bodies and souls. "Genius is the activity which repairs the decay of things."

And I am like the apple I picked and ate there at Mount Auburn that October when the leaves were falling, divinity my compost.

SONG OF DEGREES

I am very much struck in literature by the appearance
that one person wrote all the books . . .

Ralph Waldo Emerson

In the glare of two-billion-year-old light
these people stand to gain as much as they lose by their position
and they are said to eat their wives and children.
Friends also follow the laws of divine necessity.

The whole frame of things preaches
indifferency. Do not craze yourself with thinking.
The same omniscience flows into the intellect
and makes what we call genius.

They have light and know not whence
it comes. I almost wrote "no not whence,"
and why not wear it thus.

In the nature of the soul is the compensation
for the inequalities of condition. The death
of a brother assumes the aspect of a guide or a genius.
I am my brother and my brother is me.

It has been a luxury to draw the breath
of life. We were children playing with children,
playing with children. You cannot draw the line
where a race begins or ends.
I love a prophet of the soul.

She knew not what to do and so she read.
Having decided what was to be done, she did that.
No matter whether she makes shoes or statues,
or laws. It is easy to see
what a favorite she will be with history.
Her book shall smell of pines.

The poets made all the words.
The rainbow, mountains,
orchards in bloom. Stars.

Money is as beautiful as roses.
This is the meaning of their hanging
gardens, villas, garden houses.

DREAM AFTER READING PASTERNAK

Last night I dreamed that Wanda called me about community college, but her name was Lara.

Lara's favorite color was mauve the color of lilac in bud. She liked to sit in the violet dusk at the shop near the black-current caramels in glass jars that matched her favorite color.

In my dream when my mother saw Wanda she said what she always used to say. Then my mother died, and Wanda was trans-bluent, neither Union nor Confederate, neither black nor Greek. At the wake I wore mauve toenail polish, a shade called "Call Your Mother."

"Next year in Jerusalem," whispered Tip O'Neill. He was davening on the steps to the polls, counting precincts. Catholics don't daven and this is not the kind of thing he'd say but I heard it anyway.

When we were little we lived near the house where Malcolm X had lived. He stayed there with his sister when he first came to Boston. I didn't know this when I was a girl. On my desk I have a picture of his old house, a woman standing on the front porch, staring suspiciously at the camera.

In the refugee camps in Jordan where it was crowded and dry, Genet would look up at the sky: "Clouds are nutritious." In Palestine he thought of Oakland and the Black Panthers, and souls shipwrecked by the Church, and prisons and pietas. Prisons he found rather motherly.

Wanda goes to Laney, the birthplace of the Panthers, on the other side of the lake. I can almost see it from my window looking toward the Port of Oakland.

Mourning for Lara, Zhivago also mourned that distant summer when the revolution had come down to earth from heaven. Grieving, he looked at bruise-colored clouds and thought of politics. "All politics is local," said Tip O'Neill. Except for mystics.

WITHOUT SIN

Pale green carnations
Mint and lime

Filth
All gone

Incense and a linen remnant
Appealing to no conscience

Sacramental
With blood-red light

We always heard
It would be white
But it's not white

BLUE SHATTERED WINDOW

Roberta Olson

They tore down the information booth
Creating a crater
Wide enough for planets
People bury their faces in it
Angular angels with teeth
Of fence posts and dawn
All they want is directions
Without flying or taking a boat
All they want is
The feeling of the wall
As they walked out the back door
A mile of paper fallen in showers
Claims the texture of the ground
No one could understand
All this music in the air
Static rhythms pulse
With elements of speeding
You are here
It is a sunny day in August
The details of Main Street
Are trying to be elegant
The tree is in the seed
And light music moves through time
On the roadside powdery
A shadow of the world

BULGING LIKE A DREAM

The war has nothing to do with it
Houses lean and buildings are collapsing
Whether the equator bulges or not
On the threshold of autumn
A corn maze is flattened by the wind
As if it fell from the sun

Friday, writing on snowflakes
There are leaves on the stairs
The word "strewn" or a handful of pebbles
Comes to mind. In Missoula
A house takes a century to fall
When you look down
From space no ships or sea birds
Only a soft gray backdrop
Excites water to a froth
Idaho always falls
White against the sky
A buckeye butterfly spreads its wings

AMARYLLIS OUTSIDE

How long do seeds remain
In an eroded stream bed
Before the wings fold
And the feather drifts away?
In a sky of extreme purity
I had vision before sight
And pools of water everywhere
Southwest from the tower
Lies all of Polynesia
Those ruddy roses of summer
Have nothing to do with it
The rim of the world is fire
The back of the eye
Is constellated with fire
The Milky Way flows out
And paints the garden red
I feel Polynesia in my bones

IMPULSE

The praying mantis loved our water cart
Tiny white mouths
Opened at the surface for air
We made a hole in the sky
The way a drop hollows a stone
Silent as silk
Long after the storm had passed

Upright and minimal the gesture
Pulls up the arc of silence
Reflecting an image of India
With myriad forms
And hundreds of grasses

A mayfly lands on the surface
There is a new point of gravity
He raises his wing
With the elusive precision of a dream

R I P P L E

Night shreds the ocean
Into bands of light
On the black sheen
Of the worst ship in the navy
There is a sense of irony in Valparaiso
Where the sky continues, the land
Continues, the sea continues, distortion
Is the daughter of form. Like pages
The small and silken dogs surround her
They come in packs of seven
Like a charm bracelet
Or lightning seen from the sky
Details disappearing into details
Rather from the settling air
We among the ghostly voices wonder
Is this a pattern or a place?

TURBULENT MONOCHROMES

I would like to tell you
That my voice is lost
Mixing as it was
With the sound of the snow
Which melted into shadows
Where the earth cooled a concavity
That felt like my own body
When we fall and take no form
Are we no longer on earth?
Engraved in air
Gripping rocks and roots
What sets the mountains apart?
Blue is the color of light
Penetrating all the space between us
A vanishing point dissecting
The green anatomy of desire
Looking much as the world at large might
So white, so out of time, so story-like

POSTCARDS PARTOUT

He floats ethereally alone
Where a bird is always welcome
The acrobat was brilliant
Like a fish on a line
He fell into the experience of another
Where the potential exists for disaster
He will not rise entirely
Before the final fall

, , , , , , , , , , , , , , , , ,

The sudden appearance
Of a coloratura soprano
Could graphically be called
Wintry trees and kinetic
The shape of a pocket
Makes appear to migrate
Twenty-four and avid
Could you take me
To the sound of her voice?

, , , , , , , , , , , , , , , , ,

A shadow is filled
With what is not
The shape of a cat
A single Japanese iris
Scatters people to the winds
We have spent thousands
Of years chasing sunbeams

, , , , , , , , , , , , , , , , ,

She wore a green dress
That felt like the sun
A bird sitting on a branch
Is more interested in
Tranquility than power
Its song reflected from the sky
Like everything in the world
Mixed together

, , , , , , , , , , , , , , , , ,

In summer the lake
Is filled with boats
The world is full of rest areas
As you see the freeway
Is no bed of roses
Untimely appearances
By leopards and serpents
Border the little window
Beside the bed
A permanent magic
Lantern game outlines
The silhouette of our dreams

, , , , , , , , , , , , , , , , , , ,

For the twinkling lights of Le Havre
We broke sunlight into rainbows
There is a sky and the mountains
Flash like pyramids of silver
The languorous waltz of the land
Is beautiful and outlined
By a brilliant red
The first snow has fallen

, , , , , , , , , , , , , , , , , , ,

Las Vegas, where the more
Glamorous hominids wait
An hour to buy water
The land is beautiful
With a magnetic field
Shaped like a slinky
Ten years of searching
A long creek with vistas
Resulted in a constant
Change of focus - people
Cannot bring themselves to leave

SPINNING

The worst side of it all
Is that there is no worst side
Paradise when I visited
Had the properties of water
The sun cast its rays
Very yellow on the plants
Metallic greens wavering
Made everything more spiral
When we forgot to rub our eyes
I tried to describe for you
Bright slats on the floor
Made of nothing but daylight

The sentence was gold
And the ideal of real life
At the moment roughed out
A jug, a cloud, a tree
The " I " cannot be important
When our faces are assembled
When our bodies are together
When our gazes are trimmed
At the distance when
The exchange begins
When the stranger gets up
When I look at the Milky Way

ZOLA AT 62

Retirement, how ironic
Zola died of asphyxiation
The rock wall only seemed solid
It was designed
To stir things up but Zola
Found that even controversy can lead
To stagnation -- a rock in the flue
Or the sacred color in tubes
A translucent touch to both
Full of light and flesh

The headlight child finds
A new point of gravity
Looking at mountains
Thinking of light mostly looking
At one mountain. As the light
Changed the mountain changed
And the light dried his eyes
And steadied his hand his son's
Icy body turned into a strange
Enthralling subject like a mountain
Reflecting light hidden prisms
Rising like an incandescent smoke

UNTITLED

Megan Pruiett

fog bell at noon
a mirror sky

fingers feel
words' undersides

cormorants dip
through houses

dark windows
abide

back garden
sparrows busy

stems loosely tied
as if in a place

for lost things
where children

could dream
their lives

COMPOSITION

                    as if composition were a neighborhood
      we wander steeply   with borrowed verbs
                unfolding, leisurely

                    we watch the night lights
      brighten, show the shadowy
                thinking thrust deep in our pockets

           A window creaks nearby, girl flown into
      sky, her dog circling watchfully below. Swept
                    language, a space

           for dreams, the baby's scream
      of triumph. As with comparisons; little escapes
                    strays, now tasted

                    too much rich food, we say
      when longing ends

Paper lanterns hung from branches: blue, red; ribbed and filled with passing; the sidewalk afternoon. Follow inside routine; climb steps, drop a bag, make way to extract such secrets as childhood requires.

What moves through? The ways books speak in signs, smells of dust jackets or canted spines, a stray glance; circumstance; a building. At midnight the lover stood waiting, nightbirds silent in place of drunken song, argument, blue screens flickering.

Take, for example, D. leaving in tears, A. professing mistreatment at the hands of C. Or me, blue, clutching at G. As if these emotions outlast us. One by one, we encounter each other, what was left in the yard. Bright, the diagram splices quiet, blind to who?

I wonder. Opposite, green's emergence, foray for everyone. Hello, bird. O, hello, cars roaring. Between happened happens, coloring if not words, shadows.

"blindly as a poem that is written too soon" Inger Christensen
"Midnight's Gate" Bei Dao

March 27, 2010

Where were you, all those days before you died? Was there space to say goodbye? Someone said, a sweetness. Someone said. In the field, ask white to crest its black ships, sound steps along the planks. To build your end, a dark hawk; an owl's cry, unseen.

There are words for the way moss feathers as it grows or humus yields to mushrooms in wet spring; the ways leopard snails twine above the ground, suspended on a viscous string in coitus. Choices and non-choices marshaled on the shelf—someone picks up a rock. It has a name, but I don't know it. Say, basalt. Serpentine. To meet remembering.

When I die, what will speak for me? How do we mouth what isn't, windless Os ascribed no where? A frog calls, and wind. The doors are locked. What may be hums continuously, knows we feel its name.

"… and that is what poetry is, it is a state of knowing and feeling a name."
Gertrude Stein
"Is there any good in saying everything?" Basho

April 17, 2010

In memory, I stood, a great blue heron's back to me, wings spread, head to one side. Again, I heard the weight of wings as herons hove the hill, one's white feces spattering grass like paint. The light was also late.

One gives way to others, is split to fit a pattern. As that toad in dark green shade, or damp on cool cement, dark green bucket. Skin sloughs from the mind, its opaque, patterned creases, little Sunday dresses kept best in rooms for guests. Silver mirror, brush, the powder and paperbacks. Nested. How we lived lies scattered

unseen beneath the bed. Those lost are called in clearer than us not then now. Cells scry, inscribe, move on. This twilight catches other blues, ceramic glazes, pages of illuminated books. And you within me, little kick, I hold you to this name and that, lift the latch to let your stories in. Memory set swinging, you will be

a pattern changed. Sea of sunlight, scribbled page. Lamps lit in the dark.

"There is no mirror to memory" Norma Cole
"Structure   without life   is dead. // But life   without // structure   is un-seen." John Cage

April 18, 2010

I don't know where the story goes, nor where it's been. Tracing the least pattern in glass just cleaned from accreted rain.

After hearing a crash, he watched a fight ensue on the street below. I turned into a darker pillow. Doing, not-doing reverberate

past the din. Wind again, reminiscent of itself; a postcard returned from some lost place, needing to be deciphered. Without annotation, the baby moves, improbably

a coyote, on her way to somewhere else.

There is difficulty in articulating what we do, she said, and that difficulty became my own. Do, that word, planted then eaten. Nudge under thumb. Dropping suddenly, I woke

a swallow parched and clamoring. Are we all poets then, dancing with few leaves? In palmfuls of dirt, we tamp ourselves at an angle, that the rains won't toss us down.

"What we are setting out to do is to *delimit* the work of art, so that it appears to have *no beginning and no end, so that it overruns the boundaries of the poem on the page*." Barbara Guest
"Single motion which departed, leading itself by the hand." Anne Carson

May 29, 2010

come back again   soft   soft   birdsong and buses
heaving past   come back again   soft   soft   deer-broke
detritus   on the path   soft   soft   the baby is only satisfied
with bright, white noise.   come back again. apples soften with honey
muscles shift as he rotates his arm.   soft   soft   come back again
she emailed her anger at last, a scattershot report   settling slowly.
come back again.   soft   soft   mind lurches on its ride   soft
     soft   curls and uncurls   soft   soft   cat claws picking across
               a once-learned song   soft   soft   come back again
          clear days after rain   soft   bring   soft   water meeting water
               in the drain   soft soft a stretching   intention   soft
               against attention   soft   sun succumbs to blue
     come back again   soft   soft   elsewhere lies   soft   elsewhere.

                                        interrupted leaves its mark
                                                fossil record
                                          hiccup and spark
                                            silence and
                                         jostled, swayed
                              in birdsong and traffic played

LITTLE THINGS (TRIO)

little things little things little things
the difference between

memory distilled
in distance, a
jar of song

Language slippery flow cloud tablets on damp, court, child cough, quail trio teetering dark, green, four translucent drops, deer trio, oblong muscles chewing, white chins, faint warm smell. Quilted hillside. Swallow's spread tail, trill, flit. Grey-gold lost light, cypress, black stencil for blue night, the sea, textured arms-length-to-me, pocketable permeable detail, foreboding, scry. Children's high-pitched howls, sodium lights, spray-lined road, black & white striped, small & round, grey under, scalloped bright, hop from that twig gone.

what inextricable

        what steadfast

      only ideas

                      woven in

   bright   within

      locating

soft ascent

      words, winter of

   swarm

     off-white sky

AN EXCESS OF FIREFLIES

Lisa Rappoport

My mother liked to drink iced coffee
on humid New Jersey afternoons. This was long
ago, before we feared caffeine or were spooked
by the outcome of so much negligence and downright
abuse of this physical world, before we had reached the point
where anything you ate or drank or breathed might
kill you, as easily as not. Because they were ignorant,
people back then could drink coffee at all hours
without it keeping them up at night.
Maybe if they tossed and turned
they had some other explanation, like
how elusive sleep can be after a thunderstorm,
or the way an excess of fireflies
foretells a night of lying awake.

She would never make fresh coffee for her cold drink;
she only had it if some remained from the morning.
I loved the color, the soft milky brown in the dimpled
amber tumbler, cubes of ice bobbing in their murky sea.
I never learned to like the taste, or to pretend I did.

In warm weather I often have an iced mocha, the bitter
coffee masked by sweet chocolate, the color just as I remember
and my own icebergs cloistered in a narrow glass. It's not humid
here, rarely even very hot; still, far from there in time and space,
I feel the heaviness of that moist summer air, the increased gravity,
the beaded sweat on me and on the glass, the closeness, the distance.

REMORSE HITS THE ROAD

I sent my remorse on a road trip, a wanderjahr
of self-discovery. Hitchhiking through some verdant
hills, it got a ride with a long-distance trucker.
They ate cheeseburgers and fries at an all-night diner
and talked about failed relationships. My remorse
said it never stopped thinking about water
under the bridge, and who was the bridge
and who the water. The trucker confided
that he googled his exes from time to time.
Together they regretted their dismal meal
as they sped down the black macadam in the black
night with their black thoughts. After what felt
like a very short time my remorse returned home,
wanderlust sated, grateful for the new sorrows
it had acquired. I thought it had gained weight,
but tactfully I said nothing.

A GRAMMAR OF LOSS

"Death is a black camel, which kneels at the gates of all."
> —Abd al-Qadir,
> Algerian military & political leader, poet,
> 1807-1883

I. Use of the Past Tense

It is surprisingly difficult
to begin to use the simple past
(never simple) or past perfect
(far from): like the quickly-
corrected stumbles we make
in a foreign tongue,
embarrassing ourselves; but here
not only grammar but heart
resists, yearning for the present
indicative, the continued present,
the present of ongoing action
which leads to the future.

II. Synonym

When the friend has gone,
we tend to say, "She has passed,"
"He has gone on," "Dearly departed,"
"We have lost him," avoiding
the straightforward reference
to death.

III. Case

In some languages each noun
possesses a case, such as ablative
or genitive, and in this case the case
would be accusative; but whom
to accuse?

IV. Number

The verb and the noun
must conform, like to like;
but what is the correct number
of loss?

V. Dangling Participle

Leaving so much hanging, those who
still live, the conversations which seem
to continue, the unasked and unanswered
questions . . .

VI. Diagrammed Sentences

<u>I | have lost | you</u>
   | \forever

<u>You | are lost</u>
     | \to \forever
         \<u>me</u>

VII. Conjunction

Conjunctions show relationship.
What has been joined
may then be sundered.

VIII. Subjunctive Mode

Use of the subjunctive expresses
an idea as desirable, supposable,
conditional: Would that she were alive.
If only it were to turn out differently.
I wish she were here with us.

IX. Indefinite Relative Pronoun

Whatever happened had to happen.
Whichever treatment she sought
was inadequate. Whoever could
have believed it would end
like this?

for Leila

LEAPING TREE

Thirty years ago I saw the painting
hanging in the window
of a gallery that has since folded
in a chapter long closed
We await the serial's next installment
not knowing when the issue might appear
if at all

It was called The Suicide of the Tree
or a title very similar

From a cliff's edge a line of leafy trees
watched helpless as one of their number sprang
from the earth
and fell to its death
We didn't see the death, we saw the tree
midway down the high cliff;
we saw its companions left behind;
the back story was invisible;
the moment was fragmented

The descending tree's branches were lifted
slightly by momentum and uprushing wind
The speed must have been an utter shock
perhaps a pleasant sensation or at least
novel, after a lifetime of stasis

The image has never left me
The uprooted tree continually falls yet never lands
Some of its leaves may have fluttered
upward, back up to the others

ONE OF THE RIFF-RAFF REGARDS THE MOON

Behind the moon last night
there was a second moon, bluer,
and behind that I tremble to speculate;
then tonight a coppery aura on the
single moon   which gives me something
to look forward to.

Then a moon of ordinariness, that is
"ordinary" insofar as a moon may be.

Then I wasn't looking so much.

I wondered who else noticed the blue
moon, who else might affirm this
experience of unusual blueness.

I didn't ask.

FIVE SELECTIONS FROM
THE SERIES BODY PARABLES

His knee was hurting more than usual: like a sea, with waves of pain that responded to some faraway source, dim and feeble yet strong enough to exert its influence across a vast distance. As the sky darkened at the next full moon, he applied the poultice he had made of sea salt, algae, dulse, and sea urchin eggs, soaked since the previous new moon in a tincture of blue-black ink. The pure white gauze drowned in the black, salty liquid, which ran down his shin and into his slipper. Lying on the beach with his poulticed leg propped on a Styrofoam cooler, he inspected the moon's craters and seas through binoculars.

She didn't remember when she first noticed her fingernails turning pale green. They were horizontally ridged and broke easily. One hand was more affected than the other: the right, the one she used to write or draw. She pulled rusty nails from the beams of a collapsed barn, soaked them in a thickening shampoo, and buried them in the back yard by her pet turtle's grave. Two weeks later she got a new turtle and named it Nell.

It was because his heart had been bruised that he began eating rich foods. Pastries, ice cream, chocolate mousse—anything with plenty of lipids; the sugar didn't matter so much. In addition to the weight he knew he would gain, he thought he could add a layer of fat to his heart, a surrounding buffer zone which would repel any enemy fire. He had forgotten how easily a knife slices through butter.

His skin had an odd sheen, more noticeable in some lights than others. On a street after dark, when street lamps were lit, it reflected the way a sheet of glass does when you tilt it. His face always looked moist, with moisture remaining on the surface the way it does on metal. It tasted metallic too, and the aftertaste was thin and blue.

The eye does often feel like the I, especially when in pain. The Andalusian dog knew it and eye know it. Planetary bodies blink, are covered with darkness, send back light they have received. An orb can be the portal from inner to outer or from seeing to being seen. Please, Mr. Sandman. When Margaret's mother received a corneal implant, her friend told her the first thing she would see would be the last seen by the donor. They scoured the newspapers, the friend reading aloud any likely leads. The only recent local death was a man killed holding up a 7-11. Bull's-eye.

CONTINUITY

Sarah Suzor

The human embodiment
of physical perfection
exists in a profile measuring
eighty-seven degrees
from crown to brow.

Words will string and string

he explained

to sketch geometry
is different.

SECRETIVENESS

Embarrassing almost,
how intriguing it was:

subtleties,
a season's end
starting to shift,
become increasingly obvious.

Whatever went unsaid
took shape in interaction—
        the friction of air
        and a movement through it.

    , , ,

Discordant sounds gave her such pain

but how was he to know?

That look in her eye
the way her face turned toward the hills.

ESTEEM

Aspiration–
      and the muscles of the neck
      surrender their will–
acknowledge its sway.

Her contentment
contingent
on the reaction of birds,
their dealings with an hour,
in particular, a season.

Winged or not
she rises just to see them so.

SUBLIMITY

Since his position had been secured
the state of being was rendered finest

, , ,

Qualities of matter
had little to do with
the direction she was walking

, , ,

And she wrote her name
across the man on whom
the sun goes down

HUMAN NATURE

The whole is equal to
the sum of its parts
and the equivalent
of the effort,
exponential.

He was only talking
about geometrics.

, , ,

Suppose it was found:
      a way to communicate the need to adhere to an answer
      and the need to make one up.

Suppose communication was the only thing
that differentiated the two intentions.

She still doesn't sleep at night,
not with all the driving wind.

Chapter One: Expressing Remorse

Tomorrow, or the day after today,
remember something,
some time you felt comfortable enough
to put yourself in a vulnerable position.

You were probably sitting on a couch,
or walking down a quiet street.

Now picture one of the most beautiful faces you've ever seen?
Did you get to kiss them?
Did you get to hold their face in your hands
and feel like the rest of the world ceased to exist?

Did you ever take them to breakfast?

Did you ever have to tell them:
You know, I'm not proud of this,
but there's something I need to apologize for.

What was their reaction?

What was their favorite flower?

Did you ask them, or did they tell you?

Picture their house.
Their friends.
The way they laughed.

How did it end?
Good? Bad?
Scale it.
One to ten.
One being the worst. Ten being the best.

Are you ever sorry it didn't work out,
I mean, do you have remorse, regrets?

What do you say when you look in the mirror?

Do you say: I'm better off without them.
Or do you say: I wish they were never born.

What do you think they say about you?
What do you think they say about you when they look in the mirror?

Did you two have a song?
You know, something that summed up your relationship?

How does it feel to hear that song now?
The same? Different?

Scale it.
One to ten.
One being the same. Ten being completely different.

Do you ever hear that song in unexpected places, like the grocery store,
    or a shopping mall?

Do you ever play it for yourself
just because you want to feel something?

Feel sad, maybe?

Really, though,
what are some of the very first thoughts
that run through your mind
when you look in the mirror?

Chapter Two: Endorsing Reciprocity

In seven days, or a week from today,
write down a time you wronged someone.

You were probably on a tropical vacation,
or under the influence of a controlled substance.

What were your dreams the next night?

Did you wake up in a cold sweat?

If yes, were you concerned?

If no, were you concerned?

Then, picture the most beautiful face you've ever seen.

Did you offer them your phone number?

Did you say:
I don't know you, but I'd like to see you again.

What were your expectations when you saw them again?
Did you get nervous?

If yes,
did you cross your legs,
put your hand on your knee
and start to shake your foot?

If no,
did you lie to them?
Say, "I'm swamped with work right now.
I should really get back to it." And leave.

What did their mouth look like?

Did you touch their leg?

Did you ever look at their mouth,
touch their leg, and think to yourself:
I would never harm this person.

Were your intentions pure?
What does the term "pure intentions" mean to you?

Did they like coffee?

Did the two of you ever go on a tropical vacation?

Was your stay satisfactory?

Rate it.
One to ten.
One being awful. Ten being elated.

Did you sit in the sun and drink coffee together?

Did anyone else wearing a swimsuit catch your eye?

Did you think,
even for one second:
I don't know that person, but I'd like to see them again.

How did things taste after that?

Did you remind yourself of your pure intentions?

Did you put two-and-two together?

Re-evaluate?

That evening,
did you wake up in a cold sweat,
look at yourself in the mirror,
and put two-and-two together?

Stacy Szymaszek

sequent of waves albumen ferment
white cap floats hum syllables of elegy

veer anchor train to sea bottom—pendulums
Darwins of sound gull song obscure

in wide air—tintinnabular—sympathetic
under tonnage of flora ocean of phantom brain

grieve with me—Slavic Indic Arabic

James caresses

a silver fish

his eyes sunspots

against sunrise

envisions his tan arm

in a Sicilian net

gilled and thrashing

pulled by

tides so vast

they are invisible

Corsair speeds

above ancient stands

with atomic

clocks in her gut

procures a month

of daylight

midnight yelling

we see a blue arm

in the offing

firmament tears open

baring what was

our access

piratical skuas

laying claim to our islet

beat their broad wings

hold us in orbit

my injury cool

with atomized liquid

set unstable table

make myslf attractive

quill in my pocket

drink ink from China

James's feeling arm

is full — I'm

SWALLOWS WITH BANNERS

the sail menders with hands

and feet repair into dawn

trailing bolts of canvas

maneuver fish needles in half light

reach top velocity in

pantheistic celebration

let us not forget the restraints of

our vessel when in ash you enter

invertebrate sea

funnel into whalebone

form your love will seek

every plasm remembered

through my constant dream

BLACK CLOUDS. SPILLED INK

progression of centuries. drunk at night watch tower

wrote five letters

black clouds. spilled ink blotting out Balkan peninsula

pale rain. beads spatter the tarpaulin

police force wind comes. blasts and scatters them

true solar year is more than a year. pesky fraction

below night watch tower. ocean like sky

after Su Tung-Po
translated by James

spirited tars brawl sunward

one holds a reptile egg

who is too pretty to smack

holds the egg to the sun's

thermal bottom

alias James

arm

an alloy

ambidextrous

wonder

yd never

touch

POEM FOR KATHLEEN

register your
early departure
alert arms
go evergreen
note on graph
paper bound
with felt wool
personal day
radius steps
in a kitchenette
paperwhites
waft from
back room

slow-healing
toe out of mind
and gauze
as favorite concept
if antique
red cross pin
self-animated
and embedded
itself in my nouns
I would use gauze
train hands
to a firm hold
could be tartan
cloth sling
lesbian for well-being

placebo Latin
"I shall
please" you

emblems beneath
Christmas branch
looping phoenix
song St. Philomena
partially healed throat
fat from center
burning outward
old fashioned love
for the sponged out

enshrine your voice
from the Palisades
graft technology
of your voice
over my craven
ordeal a rosewood
inlay kerosene in
a cold water flat
legal where I'm from

compile oil eggs
cheese and Tabasco
in skillet do dishes
for third time
the tribulations
of Melanie Klein

balance a task
we can't live
to complete
illuminated
marital event
your Klein
and mine

I haven't much
traveled in the realms
of gold
o early and
loved people
nonchalant upon visitation
car keys plunge
over the overpass
forever in a South
Side backyard

Kathleen there is
much to worry about
this morning a screw
to my circadian
balance a Screech
Owl outside
a Wisconsin city
hides in old woods
from larger owls
the contingency
of being queer
is never to fall
in love

smoked stove drippings
the eye cares
for itself with tears
late winter art
glass send Wright's
May Basket
to Ginger
to make her day
"palatable" tying
glass ribbons into
natural light

shipment of stones
basilica dome
everyone stubborn
I in grey vest
leave industry
for something
private by the sea

the children of
my bearing years
washed away
in her cataract
none so nurtured
as her mother
atop old age
home rubble
winner of
the apocolypse

CONTRIBUTORS

MERLE BACHMAN'S Etherdome Press chapbook is *The Opposite of Vanishing*, published in 2000. Since then she has published a book of literary criticism and translation, *Recovering Yiddishland: Threshold Moments in American Literature* (Syracuse University Press, 2008) and a book of poetry, *Diorama with Fleeing Figures* (Shearsman Books, 2009). Her blog is *Orphan's Picnic* (http://merlebachman.blogspot.com/). Bachman is an Associate Professor of English at Spalding University in Louisville, KY, where she directs the undergraduate program in creative writing.

FAITH BARRETT'S EtherDome chapbook is *Invisible Axis*, published in 2001. Barrett is an associate professor of English at Lawrence University where she teaches courses in American literature and culture and creative writing/poetry. With Cristanne Miller, she coedited *Words for the Hour: A New Anthology of American Civil War Poetry* (University of Massachusetts, 2005). Her scholarly study *To Fight Aloud Is Very Brave: American Poetry and the Civil War* is forthcoming from the University of Massachusetts.

MARGARET BUTTERFIELD'S EtherDome chapbook is *Postulate*, published in 2003. Butterfield lives in Carmel Valley, California. She received her MA in Literature and Creative Writing from San Francisco State University in 1992. From 1990 to 2000, Butterfield worked for Simone Fattal at The Post-Apollo Press in Sausalito. Her work has appeared in several anthologies, including *Everything Is Real Except The Obvious* (Em Press, 1992), *Beside The Sleeping Maiden* (Arctos Press, 1997), and *Fascicles II* (Em Press, 1997). In 2010 she and her husband, Charlie Craddock, opened M42 Studio/Gallery in Carmel Valley Village where they feature his paintings as well as an eclectic group of local artists. Contact Margaret at artink@earthlink.net.

ERICA CARPENTER is the author of *Summoned to the Fences* (Etherdome, 2002) and *Perspective Would Have Us* (Burning Deck, 2006). Her recent projects have included Found Ground, a projection-based artwork involving found film footage and text, and Curiouser, a group of installations based around Victorian natural history collections, co-curated with her husband, Erik Carlson. She lives in Cranston, Rhode Island.

VALERIE COULTON is the author of *passing world pictures* from Ether-Dome (2002). Coulton is also the author of *open book* (Apogee Press, 2011), *The Cellar Dreamer* (Apogee Press, 2007), *passing world pictures* (Apogee Press, 2003), and *the lily book* (2003 Michael Rubin Chapbook, San Francisco State University). Her work has been translated into Greek and Bulgarian, and has appeared in *Front Porch, kadar koli, New American Writing, 26, Parthenon West Review,* and *e-poem.eu,* among others. She lives in Barcelona with her husband, the poet Edward Smallfield.

CAROLINE CRUMPACKER has published the chapbooks *Recherche Theories* (Etherdome Press, 2010) and *The Institution in Her Twilight* (Dusie Kollectiv, 2011). Her poetry, translations and reviews have also appeared in magazines and anthologies including *The Talisman Anthology of Contemporary Chinese Poetry* (Talisman, 2007), *American Poets in the 21st Century: The New Poetics* (Wesleyan University Press, 2007), *Not For Mothers Only* (Fence Books, 2007), and *Isn't it Romantic? Love Poems by Younger American Poets* (Verse Press, 2004). She is a member of Belladonna* Collaborative and a contributing editor for *Circumference* magazine, and was a founding editor of both *Fence* magazine and the French/American online magazine *Double Change.* She lives in "mid-upstate New York" with her lovely daughter Coco and her partner the puppeteer, Roberto Rossi. A bit further upstate, she runs The Millay Colony for the Arts, an artists' residency program.

SUSANNE DYCKMAN is the author of the EtherDome chapbook *Transiting Indigo* (2005), another chapbook, *Counterweight* (Woodland Editions, 2005), and a full-length volume of poetry, *equilibrium's form* (Shearsman Books, 2007). Her writing has appeared in a number of journals, most recently *Fact-Simile, Ambush* and the Omnidawn blog. She has been a finalist for the Ahsahta Press Sawtooth Poetry Prize and the EPR Discovery Award, and a winner of the *Five Fingers Review* Poetry Award. She lives in Albany (California) and works for a non-profit organization in Oakland.

KELLY EVERDING'S EtherDome chapbook, *Strappado for the Devil,* was published in 2004. Everding received her MFA from the University of Massachusettes, Amherst and has published poems in many journals, including the *Colorado Review, The Bloomsbury Review, Black Warrior Review, Conduit, Caliban,* and *Exquisite Corpse*. She lives in Minneapolis, Minnesota where she works for the nonprofit organization, RainTaxi, Inc., which publishes *Rain Taxi Review of Books*.

RENATA EWING'S EtherDome chapbook, *Frankenstein Poems / Somewhere West of Ideal* was published in 2008. Ewing grew up in California and Oregon, and studied creative writing at San Francisco State University. She currently lives and works for a web media company in Venice, CA.

AMANDA FIELD'S chapbook, *That Year*, was published by Etherdome in 2007. Her poems have appeared in *Ploughshares, ZYZZYVA, POOL* and elsewhere. She lives in Brooklyn with her husband, filmmaker Caveh Zahedi, and their two-year old son.

KATE GREENSTREET'S EtherDome chapbook is *Learning the Language* (2005). She is also the author of *The Last 4 Things* (2009) and *case sensitive* (2006) both from Ahsahta Press. Ahsahta will publish her third book, *Young Tambling*, in 2013.

ANNE HEIDE'S EtherDome chapbook, published in 2008 is *Specimen, Specimens*. Her poetry has appeared in *New American Writing, Notre Dame Review, Court Green, Octopus, and Xantippe*, among others. Among her many chapbooks are *Wiving* (DGP), and *Residuum::Against* (Woodland Editions, 2008). She edited the poetry journal *CAB/NET*, and is currently living in Milwaukee.

BRYDIE MCPHERSON KIUCHI'S EtherDome chapbook, *Abandon's Garden*, was published in 2000. Her poems have appeared in *Fourteen Hills, 580 Split, Bird Dog, New American Writing*, and the *Bay Poetics* anthology. She has an MFA from San Francisco State University. She is third grade teacher in San Lorenzo, and lives in Alameda with her husband and two sons.

ERICA LEWIS'S EtherDome chapbook, *excerpts from camera obscura* (2009) was created in collaboration with artist Mark Stephen Finein, as were *the precipice of jupiter* (Queue Books), and a full-length version of *camera obscura* (BlazeVox Books, 2010). lewis lives in San Francisco, where she curated the Canessa Gallery Reading Series. Her work has appeared or is forthcoming in various journals, including: *P-Queue, New American Writing, Little Red Leaves, Parthenon West Review, elimae*, *Shampoo*, *Cricket Online Review*, *alice blue*, *BOOG CITY*, *Word For/Word*, and *Try!*, among others.

SUSAN MANCHESTER'S EtherDome chapbook, *A Dress for Weather* (2009) contains poems that are born from with her many years' experience living on Santa Cruz Island, off California's coast. These lyric and shapeshifting meditations on the Lone Woman of San Nicholas Island, an indigenous woman who lived alone there for 18 years in the mid-nineteenth century, invoke the elemental rhythms and mythos of island life, its surf, seasons, and creatures. Manchester is a poet, photographer, and healer living in northern Colorado's Frontrange region.

LINDA NORTON is the author of the chapbook *Hesitation Kit* (Etherdome Press, 2007) and *The Pubic Gardens: poems and history* (Pressed Wafer, 2011). Her collages have appeared on the covers of books by Claudia Rankine, Julie Carr, and Stacy Szymaszek and are featured at Counterpath Press Online alongside her essay, "The Great Depression and Me." She has been a resident writer at the Lannan Foundation in Marfa, Texas, and at the Millay Colony in the Berkshires. "Landscaping for Privacy," her collaboration with composer Eve Beglarian, is available on iTunes. From 1987-2001, Norton worked for the University of California Press. Since 2002 she has been a senior editor at The Bancroft Library, U.C. Berkeley. Norton grew up in Boston and now lives with her daughter, Isabel Lyndon, in Oakland, California.

ROBERTA OLSON is the author of *All These Fair and Flagrant Things*, published by EtherDome Press in 2001, and *Some Numerous Dwarf Rippings* (Flash +Card press, 2007). Her work has also appeared in various literary journals including *Talisman*, *New American Writing*, *Facture*, *Bird Dog*, and *The Floating Bridge Review*. She lives in Seattle with her husband John Olson and cat Toby Olson.

MEGAN PRUIETT'S chapbook *To Music* was published by EtherDome in 2003. Pruiett concluded her two years as Affiliate Artist at the Headlands Center for the Arts in July 2010, just in time for the birth of her daughter Imogen. Her chapbook *The Naught Book* was a finalist for the 2011 Omnidawn Chapbook Contest in Poetry. Other poems have appeared, on occasion.

LISA RAPPOPORT'S 2009 EtherDome chapbook is *Aftermaths*. Rappoport is a poet, letterpress printer and book artist. Under the imprint of Littoral Press she focuses on the design and production (and often the writing) of limited edition artist's books and poetry broadsides. She finds that poetry and printing inform one another in surprising ways. Rappoport teaches letterpress printing at the San Francisco Center for the Book and in her own West Oakland studio. Her work is represented in many U.S. and international collections.

SARAH SUZOR is the author of the EtherDome chapbook *It was the season, then.* (2010), and *Isle of Dogs* (Toadlily Press, 2010). Her most recent full-length collection of poetry, *The Principle Agent*, won the 2010 Hudson Prize and was published by Black Lawrence Press in 2011. Suzor's interviews and reviews have appeared in various online and print journals including *Rain Taxi* and *Tarpaulin Sky*. Her poetry has been published widely, as well as anthologized, translated and nominated for the Pushcart Prize. She lives in Venice, California where she is the founding editor for Highway 101 Press, and a guest lecturer for the Left Bank Writers Retreat in Paris.

STACY SZYMASZEK'S EtherDome chapbook, *Some Mariners*, was published by EtherDome in 2004. Syzmaszek was born in Milwaukee, Wisconsin, in the summer of 1969 and grew up there. She is the author of the books *Emptied of All Ships* (2005) and *Hyperglossia* (2009), both published by Litmus Press, as well as numerous chapbooks, including *Pasolini Poems* (Cy Press, 2005), *Orizaba: A Voyage with Hart Crane* (Faux Press, 2008), *Stacy S.: Autoportraits* (OMG, 2008), and from *Hart Island* (Albion Books, 2009). From 1999 to 2005, she worked at Woodland Pattern Book Center in Milwaukee, where she founded and edited the journal *GAM*. In 2005, she moved to New York City, where she is the Artistic Director of the Poetry Project at St. Mark's Church.